CW00919006

To Alex.
Best wishes.
love
Jeanette Badger

This book is dedicated to my wonderful husband Chris who has given me hope, happiness and unimaginable love.

Your determination to prove to me what I could become has paid off. Throughout our time together, we have fought the hell of Post-Traumatic Stress Disorder, and countless other battles, but we have beaten them all together.

My darling, you have my heart forever, I love you. X

£1 from the sale of each copy of this book will be donated to Women's Aid

My journey from abuse, mental illness
and despair to a happier, fulfilling new life

Jeanette Badger

JEANETTE BADGER BOOKS

Printed in Great Britain by
Bell and Bain Ltd, Glasgow

Contents

Acknowledgements

To my parents: thank you for all your help and guidance over the years and for giving me the gift of life. My experiences taught me so much. You have given me the strength to fight all along the way. I love you with all my heart and always will, no matter what. Mum, I once said I wished I could give you all you ever wanted out of life … I am still trying. The support you give me is priceless. Thank you.

To my darling children: by reading my story, I hope you will all gain strength from my experiences and that this will help you through the future. I am so lucky to have had you all, and I am so proud that you are all mine. A mother's love is for life and no matter where you are and what you are doing I will be thinking of you. You have been my reason to carry my fight on. I love you all forever and no matter where I am, I will be with you.

To my brother Milton and my sister Chloe: Chloe, there were some tough times when we were growing up and I apologise if I made those times tougher for you. I love you. Milton, you really had it rough at one point in your life, but I am so proud of the way you got through it. You now have a wonderful partner and the most gorgeous children; I am so proud of you.

To Chris's mum and dad: I thank you for bringing such a lovely man into the world and for accepting me into your family as you did.

Tina, my secretary: you listened and helped me through the days when my brain surgery was looming. Instead of getting on with the job you were supposed to be doing, I had you listening to my funeral plans and arranging my will. Thanks for being there for me and never once complaining.

To Dr Parker at Worden Health Centre: what can I say about you? You gave me a kick in the right direction when I needed it. I thought you were being harsh and unkind and set out to prove you wrong, but you were absolutely right. Please keep giving me the odd little kick if you think I need it. Thank you ever so much; you are fantastic.

Manchester Care: thank you for helping me to bring two wonderful little girls into the world against great odds.

The Neonatal Unit, Royal Preston Hospital: thank you for the wonderful work you do with premature babies, and for helping mine, I don't know where we would be without your hard work and skill.

Ward 2 Royal Preston Hospital: thank you for caring for me during and after my brain surgery, you all do a fantastic job.

Ginger Homecare: you were there when I needed you. Thank you so much.

Tina at Victim Support: you promised me you would never let me down and you never did. You were there for me day and night. We shared many a sleepless night and so many tears. You will never know how grateful I am to you. You will always hold a special place in my heart. Thank you.

Alison and Annette at Domestic Advisory Services: you listened and advised me when I needed your help. You taught me so much. I will never forget what you did for me. Thank you both.

Lancashire Police Domestic Violence Officers: thank you for all the support you gave me when I needed you. You truly did help me to be safer.

Ann at Home-Start: You have been my third pair of hands and have had 50 million pairs of ears when I have felt the need to talk and to get things off my chest. We have shared a lot in the few months we have known each other, but I look forward to your visits. You are one in a million the way you give your time to families like mine. Thank you and do keep coming.

To Sue Sharp at Sharp Marketing: your help and support over the years have been invaluable. Knowing you is fun as well as being productive. Thank you.

To Frances Hackeson, Editor: thank you for all your help and advice, and for putting up with my impatience.

Thanks to Alec Price: without whose help in writing this book, I may never have achieved it. We have spent many hours laughing, drunk gallons of tea and shed a lot tears during the past few months. You said you were a person who found it hard to cry, but I got to you ... I know a good counsellor if you need one!

Preface

For years the people who knew me best and who had known of the horrors behind my life, had suggested that I write a book about my life. These people are the ones who have followed me, supported me and shared my years of poverty, bullying and abuse; right up until now – to my becoming a happily married mother of five and a successful business woman: they have seen it all.

In 2010 I was told I needed life-threatening brain surgery. Only a few months earlier, I had given birth to beautiful twin girls. Now I was facing the fact that I might not be around to see them grow up. I have three other children to consider too, and to add to the sadness of all this, two of my five children have special needs.

And what about my wonderful husband, who has given me such support for the past twelve years? He knows of everything that has happened to me. He has seen the tears and has been there to hold me and encourage me – just as I've been there for him through his fight with Post-Traumatic Stress Disorder.

Yes, it is right that I should write a book to explain to my family what I had been through and to let the world know how this ordinary woman from Leyland had come through so much and yet still had the courage to get on with life: to fight back and be the successful woman I am today.

I have been to hell and back, but as the saying goes: 'What doesn't kill you makes you stronger'! It certainly has with me. I hope this book will be an inspiration to others who have been through, or are going through similar circumstances.

The decision to call my book *Mental* wasn't arrived at

easily. I thought long and hard over titles that best suited the events that had happened in my life. I was at first going to call it *What Next?* simply because so much has happened and I keep wondering what life is going to throw at me next. Then one day while thinking about this I suddenly thought, my life has been mental, the things that have happened and the way my busy life is now, is mental too; so there you are.

The reasons for writing this book are twofold, well threefold to be honest. Firstly to highlight to others that no matter how bad things are in your life, you can overcome them. Secondly to tell my family how much I love them and how they can gain strength from my experiences. There was one more underlying reason for writing this book.

As I said, life keeps creating more and more obstacles for me to overcome and at the end of 2010 I had to undergo some very serious brain surgery that I wasn't sure I would survive. I felt at the time that I should leave a lasting record of what I had gone through in my short but very eventful life.

I hope that my book will help others who feel their lives are worthless. I want to show them that you can overcome anything: I did. If you can control the way your brain works, rather than allowing it to control you; anything is achievable. *Mental* is the story of my life. It is a story of two halves. If this book helps just one person to overcome their fears and be safe, then I will be happy, but I hope many of you will find inspiration and hope for the future in the pages that follow.

This book is a true story of my life, but I have changed some names to protect privacy.

1

From the beginning ...

In our lives we are sometimes faced with taking a look back at the most fearful events that we have chosen to avoid due to the fact that they are often too painful and too hurtful. We tend to tuck them away for as long as we can in the hope that we can cope with all the other everyday stresses and strains of life, but we don't cope, and the underlying problems that we have chosen not to face up to are always there, niggling away, and every now and again they come back to haunt us. Sometimes taking a step back and facing our demons is the only way forward. Sometimes we have to do this to get the answers we need, no matter how painful it may be to break down the walls we put up.

One of the worst periods of my life (and there have been many!) came when I was around the age of twenty-four or five. Thinking back, it turned out to be a huge turning point in my life.

Try to imagine if you can, not being able to do the simplest of tasks without it being a huge effort. I was twenty-four years old with three children. It was a struggle even to bathe myself; I couldn't even pick up my four-year-old daughter. I had carers coming in for two or three hours every day to help me bathe and to do my hair. They also helped with the housework and to prepare meals when I was feeling so ill that I couldn't. I was extremely grateful for their help.

But I was losing my dignity and it was awful to have to rely on this kind of help at my age. We had already had the bathroom converted into a shower-room with a seat for me for when I was too weak to stand, and we'd had a stair lift installed. But why – what was wrong with me? I honestly thought I was dying and was sure the doctors were missing something. I was convinced there was something seriously wrong with me.

I had been going backwards and forwards to the doctors for ages. I had already been diagnosed with having a severe bowel dysfunction, high cholesterol, pernicious anaemia, arthritis and a heart condition. I had put on lots of weight; I am only 5ft 2ins and I was weighing 16 stone. I had hit rock bottom.

My youngest child, Carrie-Ann was extremely loving and caring and giving towards me. She loved getting on the stair lift with me for a ride just so she could be close to me.

Deep down I knew I had to get to the bottom of what was wrong with me. I would sit and wonder how worried my children must be. I needed answers. I needed the doctors to diagnose me and find out what was wrong. Cancer was constantly on my mind. I was only in my twenties, and I'd had a pretty rough life up to that point. I wanted to be saved from death. I just felt that life had far more to offer me. I had to get better and find that better life for my partner and my children – and for myself.

I pleaded with my doctor to help me. I'd had more blood tests and they had proved inconclusive, yet I knew there was something wrong. Nobody could be this ill and not have something seriously wrong with them. I didn't tell my doctor about my cancer fears. I kept it to myself because I thought he would laugh at me and call me silly, but to me, it was all so very real. All I had ever wanted was to have a happy, loving life, a normal life; like other women have with their families.

There were other things that compounded these problems and added to the stress. My partner Chris, who is now my husband, was going through a very bad time of his own. He was suffering from Post-Traumatic Stress Disorder (PTSD), a severe form of mental illness. Chris had been in the army for ten years and had experienced some events that he found impossible to talk about. He had also been married previously and had two children from his first marriage.

It was a really difficult time for Chris. He had attempted suicide on a number of occasions and I felt that my own illness might be making him ill. He was very poorly and I can't describe how desperate I felt, watching him and worrying. I was so afraid of losing him. The fear of him committing suicide was awful. Chris became so ill that he had to go away in the end for assessment. The doctors found the problem and he began the long haul to recovery.

I was in the doctor's surgery, completely heartbroken and begging him to find out what was wrong with me. But the doctor said it was all in my head.

'Jeanette, you need to sort out the issues in there before you will get any better.'

I didn't believe him.

'How can you say that?' I sobbed. 'How can it all be in my head? I can understand everything; I'm not mental you know! I can think for myself. It's my body that won't work. How can I do that when I believe my head is fine?'

At that point I got the feeling that he didn't think I could sort my head out. I had got into a rut – too far gone in the head, my doctor thought! I left the room angry and feeling let down, but I was determined to get to the bottom of it. When I do find out they've missed me having a serious condition, they're for it, I thought to myself. I set out on a mission to prove my doctor wrong.

I found myself looking back at events that had happened in my life; events that could possibly have upset my life-balance and may have affected my mind in some way. I looked at the causes of mental illness, and wondered if there was any connection with what my doctor had said might be wrong with me. I thought of all the violence that had happened in my life.

I'd had a really bad time with my first husband. I started to question if it had been the bad times as a child and the bullying at school that had driven me into the arms of such an evil man as the man I had married. There was also the sexual abuse and the drugs. All that must have had some effect on my state of mind. How could I start to come to terms with all this, and where would I begin?

But the more I thought about it, the more it all made sense. I knew I had to face these problems and look them in the eye. It was by doing that, that I could possibly begin to live and have a fresh start, but there had been so much bad in my short life that I found it very hard to know where to begin.

I didn't have the best of starts in life and if I'd known what the next twenty-odd years were going to throw at me I'd probably have opted to stay in the womb. The whole nightmarish episode began even before I was born.

My mum and dad were very young and going out drinking with his pals often seemed to be far more important to my dad than spending time with his pregnant eighteen-year-old wife. Violence was often a result of the drinking and Mum said that she had come close to losing me on more than one occasion thanks to Dad's fists and sometimes even his feet.

The night before I was born was a really bad night for my mum. My dad had come home worse for wear and started all his usual threats and accusations towards Mum, and because there was no food ready, he flipped. But the reason there was no food wasn't my mum's fault.

They were living in a beaten-up old caravan that had no heating, and Dad preferred spending his money in the pub to buying a bottle of gas or providing food. So they hardly ever had any hot food anyway. My mum told me that she often only had dry Cream Crackers to eat.

This was the night of 27th July 1977; Dad had come home drunk and yet another domestic broke out, but this time he went one step too far. The fighting and probably the shock sent my mum into labour. Seeing this happen must have sobered my dad up a bit, and he phoned for the ambulance and my mum was taken to Chorley Hospital. Her labour wasn't too long and the delivery was normal. I entered the world at 2 o'clock in the morning on 28th July 1977.

Like a lot of women who experience domestic violence, she didn't report him, and didn't tell anyone at the hospital what had happened either. Whether or not they suspected anything untoward is anybody's guess. My mum was in Chorley Hospital for three days before being discharged. Those three days at least gave her time to rest and to get some decent hot food inside her. She knew when she got back to that horrible cold caravan that things wouldn't be easy, and she couldn't see my dad's habits changing just because he now had a daughter to look after.

The caravan was parked on some spare land at the back of Tracey's Garage, just off the A49 Wigan to Preston road, on the outskirts of Leyland. Mum and Dad had got together very young; both of them were only eighteen, although my dad was a few months older than my mum. At that time neither of them had much money, but they wanted to be together. The caravan provided that chance so they took it. It was only ever supposed to be a short-term arrangement.

It was fine for the first few months and then I came along and although it wasn't all that warm, it wasn't too bad during July and August, but as the nights started to draw in and the weather was getting colder, something had to change.

Mum and Dad had applied to the council for a council house. They had hoped that now they had a child it might help them move up the list, but nothing was coming up, and by the end of September it was starting to get a lot colder.

My grandma reluctantly offered to let them move in with her. This was in itself a minor miracle. She had no time for my dad, knowing what he'd been like with my mum. Grandma threatened that if he didn't change his ways he'd be out and his feet wouldn't touch the ground, but mum would only agree to the move as long as Dad could come too.

The house was a two-up, two-down terraced on the Wade Hall estate in Leyland. It was only a very small narrow street; probably only about ten houses on either side. This house was where my mum had been raised as a child.

We moved in there on a short-term basis, and from what Mum and Grandma have told me, Dad was thrown out time and again for fighting with my mum. My grandma, who was an average-sized lady, often got in between them. Mum and Dad were only small by comparison and I'm probably taller than both of them. The police were called more than once, but nothing was ever done. In those days the police tried to avoid getting caught up in domestics. The law and the police's attitude to domestic violence are different today.

Once my grandma's husband took his air rifle and shot my dad as he was running away from the house. He had always had a gun; this was something that stemmed from his time in the army during the Second World War. My mum told me that he used to fire the airgun and hit my dad in the bum.

There was another incident when my aunty Vicky had come round and Dad was arguing with Mum over what bit of money there was. My dad wanted it to spend in the pub, but Mum wouldn't give it to him because she needed food for me. He started pushing my mum whilst she was holding me and she accidentally dropped me – I was only a few weeks old at the time. My aunty Vicky ended up chasing him out of the house with a knife. My dad never had things entirely his own way where my mum's family was concerned.

We were only there for about two or three months before Mum and Dad got a council house on the same estate in Leyland; it was again a terraced house. This was quite a tight poverty-stricken area at the time. It was bad with drugs and violence on the streets in the evenings. There was even a murder on the estate around that time. It wasn't the sort of area you'd want to walk around at night.

It's different today – I can do that now, but in the late seventies, early eighties it was very different. Strangely, some of the neighbours who were there then are still there today. They were generally very kind to me and Mum, knowing what was going on in our house.

Times were very hard for us and because of Dad's drinking, the debts were mounting up. There were a few times when mum had put fifty pence in the electric meter that dad would rob it to go to the pub.

Around this period, my mum had managed to get herself a job in the local Co-op store and dad would be at home, supposedly looking after me, but many a time she would come home and find me in my cot; I'd not had my nappy changed all day and was crying.

It's odd, but as small and young as I was then, I can remember standing up in my cot and looking down the landing through the open door and screaming. It got to the point where Mum had to change her shifts at the Co-op to make sure I was looked after.

My dad did get a job working for a local blacksmiths down Moss Side in Leyland. He later trained as a roofer and one of the people he worked with was my Uncle Ralph, who later set up his own roofing business. After he'd been there for a while, my dad was doing so well that my uncle decided he would bring my dad into the business. Eventually, my uncle even integrated my dad's name into it, and they became quite successful. But things didn't really improve much at home. Some days my dad and uncle would only work until dinnertime and then they'd spend the afternoon in the pub.

During the early eighties, they could earn as much as £1,000 for doing a roof, and that was a lot of money in those days, but most of Dad's share went in the bars. My uncle was bad, but wasn't as bad as my dad. They could both have been very wealthy people if they hadn't gone down that route.

Things were so bad at home that my mum still had to claim benefits to make ends meet. My dad was taking all the money from the house, including her wage and the family allowance that was supposedly for my upkeep. He would then give her just £2 a day to live on. With that she was expected to run the house, feed and clothe me and herself, and he expected his tea on the table when he got home.

Mum was still surviving some days on dry Cream Crackers. Dad would come home from the pub, have his tea and Mum would have to have his clean clothes ironed and ready for him to go out again for the night.

There was one time when I was only little, but I can still remember vividly: I was toddling up and down the living room with my drinking cup and because I was so unsteady, the drink was spilling and I accidentally splashed it onto his best trousers, the trousers he was going out in that night. He went mad; he got hold of me and pasted me. I remember my mum shouting at him to stop and told him never to lay a finger on me again. I think for a minute she forgot herself and forgot about Dad's temper. He grabbed hold of her and pushed her up against the door and beat her.

There were lots of incidents like that, where I would be in bed and I could hear the banging and shouting, and Mum crying in the bedroom and I knew it was trouble. My mum was very fearful of my dad, she was always on edge, and she would be quite short with me too sometimes.

My crying a lot as a child must have been upsetting for her, but this was usually out of hunger and nothing more. A child needs a lot of snacks and things during the course of the day, but there was hardly ever any food in the house. There were never any sweets or treats and I would often have to make do with a slice of bread or a cracker like mum did.

The fights were sometimes so bad that our next door neighbour, Mr Sharples would come running into the house and sort out my dad. My dad was good at hitting my mum, but would never have hurt other people such as Mr Sharples, even though he was only an average-sized man and getting on in years. He is still around today and well into his eighties.

My dad's violent ways got him into a lot of trouble, including a time when he was sent to prison for armed robbery. He had robbed a travel agents. There was an incident just before he got caught for this crime where my mum had taken me out to the shops in my pushchair, and when we got back my dad went absolutely ballistic. Mum had only been pushing me around the streets with me sitting on top of thousands of pounds of cash from the robbery. Dad was frantic and my poor mum got another pasting for this, even though she had no idea the money was there.

It wasn't long after that happened that dad was caught and was put away for three years. He served about eighteen months of his sentence. During this time my mum would leave me with lots of different people while she went out with her friends. I've asked my mum about this, because I dimly remember that there was one occasion when I had been left with a man. For some reason or other

I had the idea he was called Charlie. This particular night I remember this man had the curtains drawn and there were lots and lots of police outside, and they were knocking at the door. We sat behind the curtains and hid, but all the time we were there this Charlie person was touching me down below. I was only three at the time, but I can remember not liking what was happening. When my mum came home that night he told her that the police had been around looking for him, and he told her he had hidden until they'd gone.

Some years later, my mum told me when I asked her about this incident, that he had been hiding from the police because they were looking for him for abducting a girl the week before. My mum had found him with the girl at our house. She gave her money to get home with, and when she got home the girl reported him.

I didn't know at the time but he was my dad's step-brother. I didn't tell my mum about him touching me. After he left, I didn't see him again for many years, until I went looking for my nan; my dad's mother. But when I did meet him again, I didn't like him. I didn't know it was the same man: it was only when I learnt his name was Charlie that I asked my mum about him and found out he was my dad's stepbrother, but I know I never felt comfortable around him.

During the period when Dad was in prison, as I explained, my mum was leaving me with anybody and everybody, there were lots of 'uncles' around and some of the babysitters were just young kids. The house had become very run-down and there was graffiti all over the walls. People would write silly messages on them, like: 'Carol's gone to the shop'. We found the messages years after when we stripped the walls to re-decorate.

We had been given blankets by Social Services and they were horrible coarse things, like they were made out of horsehair. We could never afford toilet paper, we had to use old newspapers. The carpets in those days were worn down to the hessian and even appeared to have a black tar-like substance all over them. As my mum tells me about those days, because I was so young and obviously can't remember very much, she recoils at the thought of how we used to live.

I can remember my bed having barely any stuffing in the mattress and the coil springs sticking through. In fact there was about a one-metre square part of the mattress that had absolutely no filling. The house was always freezing cold. We never had any heating in the house because Mum couldn't afford to pay the bills. The electricity and gas had been cut off so we had to light the rooms with candles at night. It seemed to be like that for years; I suppose at the time it was normal to me as a child.

Some of my babysitters at that time were really nice and one in particular, Tracy, was lovely. She used to take me to the park and we'd look for chestnuts and roast them on the fire. Sadly Tracy died in her forties; she had gone on to get involved heavily in drugs, as did a lot of people around our way at that time.

My mum told me that when Dad came out of prison he had some money. He must have been in a very good mood. I was just coming up to my third birthday. He gave her some money to treat me and to give me a birthday party. She had £20 to spend – it was a lot of money in those days and certainly a lot for my mum to have.

We went to the local shops on Wade Hall, and mum began to pile all these goodies into a big black bin bag. Crisps, cakes, biscuits, sweets and even pop – the lot went into this big black bag. Now, nobody goes shopping with a bin bag, but my mum did that day.

I can remember the day he came home, we were waiting for him. We knew the day he was being released, and I was very excited. My mum was quite nervous, not knowing what to expect, but he seemed different. Maybe he'd had time to think and he appeared to feel quite guilty in some respects. He must have missed me while he was in prison, he'd drawn a picture of me that was really like me and said to be very good, but to this day no one knows where the picture went.

However, it wasn't long before he was back to his old ways, going out drinking, and Mum had a lot more beatings from him. Then in 1980, my mum became pregnant again and on 2nd August 1981 along came my brother Milton. This was to cause more bitterness and fights. Because Milton had blond hair and my dad was very dark, he would continually accuse my mum of having had an affair.

A lot of this was done as an excuse to get out of the house and he would often disappear for days on end. My mum knew he was womanising. She even ended up catching sexual diseases from him because of his sleeping around.

I can recall my aunty telling me about a time my mum went round to her house and she could hardly move. She had gone round to Aunty Vicky's house because they were very close, and my aunty knew about my dad and the problems my mum was having.

My aunty Vicky said to mum, 'Let me have a look.' What she saw was awful. She said things were growing out of her down below, and that this was a serious sexual disease. My mum had to have treatment from the doctor. But she had to be treated on the quiet, because if Dad had found out he would have blamed it all on Mum. He would have accused her of having affairs, when it was probably his messing around that had caused this.

There was a period when Mum took me, left home and moved in with Aunty Vicky, her husband and their two children. My dad would come around and try to get us back, but he was quite wary of Aunty Vicky. She wasn't such a big woman, not tall by any means, but she was feisty and wouldn't stand any messing from anyone. She was certainly harder than my mum. My mum definitely felt much more comfortable and safe there.

My aunty had a lovely home. It was a council house but it was always kept nice and there was always food on the table even though her husband was one of the men who my dad worked with on the roofing job, and they would go to the pub together, but my uncle knew when to stop and he and my aunty had a good solid relationship. She also wouldn't take any rubbish from him

As with everything else, my mum was soft, and after a while Dad managed to talk her round into going back home to Wade Hall, but there were many more fights and we would end up back at Aunty Vicky's. We had some good times there. In the summer we would go off to a place we called Strawberry Fields which was on Southport Road. You could go into the fields and pick your own. I thought this was great because you could eat them as you were going round picking and for a four-year-old, this was heaven. I used to be covered in pink juice from the straw-berries. My aunty would make all kinds of things with the strawberries once we got them home.

Being there also gave my mum a bit of freedom. Aunty Vicky knew my mum hadn't had much of a life, so one year when the local fairground came to Leyland, my mum left Milton with my aunty and took me with her and some of her friends to the fair. By this time she had been away from my dad for quite a long time and although he had kept coming round and trying to get her to go back, she wouldn't go. He had even broken into the house on one occasion and forced himself on her, probably hoping she still felt something for him. But mum wanted to do some-thing with her life; she had been bullied and oppressed for a long time – far too long!

I thought the fair was great, but my mum and her pals would insist on taking me on all the adult rides and this was very scary for me – a four-year-old! But I went along with it. That night, my mum met a man called Sean from the fair and she took quite a shine to him. I think she saw him again while the fair was in Leyland.

She heard a short while later that the fair was going to be in Blackburn and I think Sean had asked her to go along there. She must have asked my aunty if she could leave Milton with her while she went over to stay with him, taking me with her. My aunty agreed.

The fair was being held at Witton Park, Blackburn. It was Easter time and I remember it was still pretty cold. Mum met Sean and we stayed with him. He was living in the back of a huge fair lorry. There was a large separate compartment at the back of the driver's cab and in it there were two bunk beds and a large flat area underneath. Mum and Sean slept in the bunk beds and I slept on the flat bit. Also staying in the lorry was my mum's friend, Alice who was seeing Sean's friend, a black man.

It was great being part of the fair. I was having quite a good time: I was with the fair people and they loved having me around, being a child. I pretty much had the run of the place and could stay up late. Everyone was friendly and I was the centre of everything that was going on, and of course I was with my mum.

We'd been there for about three or four nights and every night when we got into the lorry and settled down for the night, my mum would always ask Sean, 'Are all the doors locked?' and Sean always assured us they were.

But on this particular night my mum had asked, again, 'Are the doors locked?' Sean said they were and we went to sleep.

Then later that night – I don't know what time it would have been – I was wakened by men shouting. I think there were three of them. They had burst into our lorry and were attacking my mum. I can remember it so vividly. One of the men got hold of me and put a gun to my head and was telling my mum and the others in the lorry 'I'm going to shoot her; I'm going to shoot her.'

I was crying and obviously very afraid. The man was dragging me out of the doorway of the lorry. He had his hand over my mouth trying to stop me from making a noise. I instinctively bit his hand and he dropped me to the ground, which seemed a long way down. I scooted under the lorry and hid behind the huge wheels, terrified and unable to do anything.

I sat there for the rest of night. I could hear my mum and the others screaming and shouting, and the three men threatening that they would shoot someone. It was absolutely freezing; there was even snow on the ground, but I was too scared to move.

Later that morning – it was just coming daylight – I heard a generator starting up on a burger van and saw the lights come on. I ran to the van and banged on the door. When I told the man what had happened he came over to our lorry, and by this time my mum was wandering around looking for me and trying to find her clothes.

I can remember another man called Mark went looking around for my mum's underwear and clothing. He came back with some of it, but not all of it and I remember my mum's friend's bra had gone. There was a lot of commotion around the site that morning, but there was no sign of the three men. After a while my mum said she was leaving and she wouldn't be back again. Mark asked her where she would go and she told him 'Back to Leyland.'

We had very little money. We tried to find a phone box to ring for a taxi, but couldn't find one and we ended up hitch-hiking to Leyland. My mum wasn't sure whether or not Sean and his mate were involved in the rape. She had no way of proving it, but she always suspected they might have been.

Quite a while later, it was in the news that a young woman had been raped and murdered on a fairground in

Southport. Three men had been arrested and convicted for that crime. My mum often wondered if these were the same three men, but the night it happened to her it was pitch black and she didn't see their faces.

By this time my dad had left home and had given up on Mum. We still had the house on Wade Hall. He was living in Preston with his new girlfriend. Things were still fraught between my mum and dad where I was concerned. My mum now had a new man in her life, a man she later went on to marry. His name was Mark and he was the man from the fairground in Blackburn, who had been so kind to my mum that day. Mark had come over to Leyland to see my mum and to see if she was OK. They got on very well and their relationship developed.

My dad still cared for me very much; he would come over to Leyland to see me and Milton, but more for me than Milton. Dad still had this thing about Milton and his blond hair, but anyway he would come over at the weekends, pick us up and take us to the pub and to the playground for the afternoon.

It got to the point where I began to miss him so much and I never wanted him to go at the end of the visits. I then began to create and cry saying, 'I want my dad, I want my dad ... I want to go and stay with him.'

It got so bad that in the end I went to stay with him and his new girlfriend, Abbi, for a while. My mum didn't have the fight left in her to argue at that point and she let me go. But after a year had gone by, she decided I had to come home and she went to court to get me back. My time with Dad and Abbi hadn't been all that rosy either. I think my dad must have been violent with her as well, but I never saw the violence.

When I first moved in with my dad and Abbi, I used to try to do all sorts of little jobs for them. I think I did this because I wanted to please them and be liked, but it then got to the point where Abbi would expect me to do things and take me for granted.

She had a little boy of her own called Sam. She once hit me and busted my nose. It was one morning and I was late for school. She told me to take Sam to the toilet and I said no because I was late. She punched me on the nose and there was blood everywhere.

She begged me not to tell my dad, but I did. Thinking about it, I think she must have been fearful of my dad. My dad was out at work: he was still working with my uncle on the roofing jobs. When he came home from work I told him; he just said to me, 'Go outside and play Jeanette.' So I did as I was told.

I think my dad must have had a quiet word with Abbi, in his own way, because things changed after that; it didn't happen again. It wasn't all bad, though, sometimes I was spoilt rotten at my dad's. My dad gave me everything while I was there.

He was working and he was also spending more time at home with Abbi rather than going to the pub like he used to – Abbi was a very attractive lady. My dad would bounce me up and down on his knee to the music and sing to me calling me his little Caribbean Queen, which made me feel so special.

Christmas at my dad's was very good. I remember this particular year my aunty Vicky had sent me a present. It was some knickers that had a different day of the week on each pair: Sunday, Monday, Tuesday, Wednesday, Thursday, Friday and Saturday. I had a different pair for every day! I'd never had so many knickers and I was in my element. My mum sent me a 'My Little Pony' and my dad went mad saying, 'Is that all she can send?' but I wasn't bothered. At least I'd got something.

When it came to the point where my mum wanted me back home, she found the courage to go to court. At the hearing the judge ruled in Mum's favour and my dad was told he had to hand me back to my mum. When my dad came home from the court hearing, I was upstairs and I could hear him telling Abbi that he had been told to arrange a time to take me back. He said to her that he wasn't going to do it; he wasn't going to let me go and he would run away with me before he'd do that.

I heard all this and was worried that he would get into trouble. I remembered his being in prison once before and didn't want him to end up there again, so I started to cry and told him I wanted to go back.

He said 'No, you're not going back.' I said, 'I am, I am, I am!' He smacked me, then he broke down in tears in front of the fire and realised he had to take me back.

He took me as far as the shops on the Wade Hall estate, which were just around the corner from where we lived. He hugged me, gave me a kiss and dropped me off. We were both upset.

I didn't see him for a few weeks then it was my birthday – as usual everyone at home had forgotten, but there was a knock at the door and a girl brought a message that Dad was waiting outside the shops with some presents for me in his car. Mum refused to let me go to him – I was devastated.

Later that year, it was a dark November evening and I was coming back home from my aunty's house when his car pulled up alongside me. He said he was moving away from the area and that he wanted me to go with him. I panicked and shouted at him to go away. I ran home and told my mum that Dad had tried to grab me, but he hadn't, he'd just asked me if I wanted to go with him. I can still hear the last words I said to him: 'Go away, I hate you and I never want to see you again!'

He went, and I didn't see him again for many years. I hadn't said it because I meant it. I'd said it because I didn't want my dad to go to prison again for taking me away, but I had to live with that guilt for a very long time.

2

Starting school

Before I'd gone to live at my dad's I'd already been at school for a couple of years, and with all the upset and upheaval that had gone on in the early years of my life, I had been ready for school. I'd hoped it would make me like the other kids at last.

I was very excited at the thought of starting school, especially the idea of meeting new friends and having a playtime, and of course the food was great. I started school at the age of four years and two months, at St Andrews Infants School, Woodlea Road, Leyland. My cousin Lucy started at the same time as me. Lucy was a few months older than me. Little did I know how it was really going to be though. The kids there were pretty cruel – even at that very young age they could be so nasty. The fact that we were supposed to have a uniform didn't enter my head. I didn't think about that sort of thing – I was only four after all, but compared to the others I had odd uniform; nothing matched and I was picked on and called names because of this.

My cousin did stick up for me, but it didn't stop them. She was put down too in for being with me, but she did become quite popular later.

I was called smelly and all sorts of other names I didn't understand at that age, and picked on for being dirty or having odd socks and wearing the same clothes for days on end. And I remember the boys and girls would play games like 'kissy catch' and the boys would say things like, 'Don't kiss her', meaning me, but I would run around hoping that I would get caught. There was an occasion when a boy felt so sorry for me he secretly held my hand under the desk. I thought he was really kind. He was quite a popular lad himself, and he used to smile at me. He could see I was unhappy, with my head down quite a lot. I was really impressed with him. His name was Richard Forshaw.

At playtime hardly anyone would bother with me, and I remember saying to the other kids one day, 'Well Richard held my hand', and all the kids went 'Ugh! Don't hold her hand; she's got warts and your hand's going to drop off now.'

I did have a problem with warts at that time. I don't know if it had anything to do with my playing in the brook and trying to catch frogs. I had this thing for tadpoles and I would go off and play in the brook near our house. I would come home wet through, but I didn't care. I loved getting my hands in the water and going underneath the banking catching fish and frogs. But after the other kids had said that to Richard he didn't hold my hand again.

I was at St Andrews Infants School for the first two years of my school life before moving up to Woodlea Primary. It wasn't all bad at St Andrews and the teachers were good to me. They could see that there were issues at home. I do remember one teacher in particular who was so lovely towards me, Mrs Melody; she was always smiling and looked out for me. There were times when the other kids would say things like, 'It's her fault, it's her fault Miss' and she would say, 'No it isn't, it's your own fault', because she knew that I was getting picked on.

She would often just let me go off to play. There was an area next to the classroom that was fitted out like a kitchen and I was allowed to play in there quite often.

My education wasn't going too well, probably because of the things that were going on at home and with the other kids making my life a misery as well, so I was far happier just playing on my own in the playroom, and Mrs Melody knew that.

We used to have school plays but I was never picked for a part. I suspect it was because my mum couldn't afford the costumes, but there was one time when I was chosen. Mrs Melody had made me a costume. She'd done it all for me. I played the part of an angel.

Mrs Melody was a lady in her late forties, a tall thin lady with very long fingers. She didn't have any children of her own, or not that I knew of anyway. She was such a wonderful lady. At our assembly there would be the teachers who did all the talking, but it was Mrs Melody who played the piano and she was so good, she always had a smile on her face, and she had a wonderful voice. I used to sit near to the front just to be near her, she was so jovial. And she could see I was smiling.

At the other end of the spectrum, there was one teacher – I think her name was Mrs Howe – who frightened the life out of me. Not that she ever did or said anything to upset me, it was just the way she was. She was the sort who didn't take any nonsense from anyone. She used to walk really fast everywhere she went. And she only had one arm, but she always had the sleeve dangling down and flapping around instead of being tucked into her cardigan, and I remember this flapping sleeve used to scare me, I don't know why.

She seemed so strict to me. She was really probably quite a nice lady, but as a child this empty sleeve waving around uncontrollably frightened me. It's weird really what goes through your mind as a child.

On my last day at St Andrews, Mrs Melody sat me down next to her, put her arm around me and she told me not to allow all the bullies to upset me. She said she couldn't wait to see me again. But she said that probably wouldn't be until I was taking my own children to school.

After I had moved up to Woodlea Junior School I used to go over to the fence on our playground, where it backed onto the infants, and sometimes I would see Mrs Melody and wave to her. But unfortunately, that wasn't so often because she would generally do the dinnerlady duties, so she didn't come out into the playground so often.

I will go and see her again soon. I asked about her a couple of years back and I was told that she still goes back to the school for the school leavers' days. I know she will remember me: she always said she would never forget me, and I will never forget her, she was such a wonderful lady.

I hadn't been at Woodlea for very long when I went over to Preston to be with my dad. I was away for a year or so. I didn't know what to expect at Woodlea. I didn't know if it would be strict, but one thing that stuck in my mind was the smell of that school compared to St Andrews. It smelled unclean in some way, even though it wasn't. It's hard to explain.

But one smell that I thought was absolutely out of this world was the food smell. I couldn't wait for dinner. There was a board on the wall outside the hall that had the menu on it. And boy, could I eat! I was so small and thin, I think the teachers wondered where I was putting it all, because I would go back for seconds and thirds and more some-times; but I had to stock up, because I knew I would be lucky if I got anything at all when I got home.

Straight away the new children were having a go at me, calling me a tramp and things like that. I had hoped it would be different being at a new school, but I forgot that some of the kids I'd been with at St Andrews had fol-lowed me to Woodlea and word soon spread. My uniform situation was no better and there was no money for new clothes.

However, when I came back there after being at my dad's for a year I did go back with new uniform and for a while things were easier, but it wasn't long before my new clothes were getting tatty, and then the bullying started again.

There was one girl who I got on with called Claire, she lived on the same estate as me and would walk home with me. This lasted for a while until she became popular with the other boys and girls, and then she stopped walking home with me for fear of getting bullied herself. My cousin Lucy went off with her too. We had always been pretty close, but she was getting bullied as well for being with me.

There was another game, very similar to kissy catch, where all the boys would line up in a row and all the girls in another row. One by one the boys would go down the line and see how many girls they could kiss in a certain time. Although I didn't really like playing this game, I used to line up with the rest. I suppose in a way I was secretly hoping things might change and someone might like me, but it didn't happen and all the boys avoided me and kissed all the other girls. They used to say, 'You can't be kissed, if we kiss you we'll die!' and they would call me a tramp.

I can laugh about it now, but I used to cry my eyes out at being constantly rejected. There were two little alcoves in the corners of the walls of the school and I very often used to hide away in these alcoves; I felt safe there and thought nobody could see me, and when I'd been put down at games I'd run back to my alcove and cry.

There were a few times when I'd be hiding there and the kids would come to the alcoves and pull my hair and spit on me and kick me. It was horrendous, but I never once fought back or tried to hit them. I'd stay there hiding.

The dinnerladies soon became aware of this. One lady in particular knew what was going on and would chase them off. She was a fairly short stocky lady and I remember she had a very high-pitched voice. All the kids used to have a go at her too. I think that's one of the reasons she looked out for me. She would tell them off for picking on me and they would call her names and say things like, 'Oh, get lost Fatty'. She had a strange way of walking and reminded me of a bulldog the way she strutted about. She was a strong lady and she would wait for me sometimes and walk around the playground holding my hand. She very often had a lolly in her pocket for me at playtime. This is another lady who I still think about today, and wonder how she is.

In the school in those days, we had dinnerladies and then there was a head cook, and our head cook was Mrs Sharples our next door neighbour. She was well on in her years even then and couldn't have been far off retiring. Luckily for me she was in that school for as long as I was, and she used to say to the other dinnerladies, 'Make sure Jeanette gets plenty – give her whatever she wants.'

I was very fortunate that these women could see the circumstances and the background I came from. They knew there was poverty in my family. I didn't need asking twice if I wanted any more, especially for the desserts. I would go for fifths and sixes given the chance. Chocolate pudding and green mint custard – Oh my God, did I love that? And semolina with jam!

I would eat so much it is a wonder I didn't pop, but it was surprising how quickly it wore off in the playground once I got running around. Mind you I had to be careful running around because my shoes, or pumps as they were, used to talk to me. The sole was hanging off and it used to flap when I walked. But we were so poor that I just had to make do with them.

There was one instance when I'd found a really cool pair of my stepdad's trainers, I think they were Nike ones, and I decided to wear them for school. The only thing was, they were a size seven and I only took a size three, but I wore them anyway and I thought I looked so good.

After the Christmas holidays we would go back to school, and everyone would be asking what you'd got for Christmas – I would make up all sorts. I was such a liar! I would say I'd got this and that, but none of the other kids would ever believe me and they used to tell me to bring it in to school to prove it.

It was the same after the summer holidays. All the kids would be saying where they'd been and I would make up stories that I been to places that I'd only heard of on the telly. I'd say I'd been to Paris or Rome, places like that. I even used some of my mum's fake tan one year to make it look like I had been abroad; I was tangerine when I went to school. What a loony! I didn't tell the tales because I was an out and out liar, it was just because I wanted to fit in with the rest of them, but they knew what I was saying wasn't true and in some ways it just made the situation worse for me.

The bullying and the name-calling were never-ending, and no matter how I tried to be friendly with the other kids it made no difference. I was known as 'The Tramp' and it hurt. All I ever wanted was to be liked and to be part of the crowd.

It wasn't long after I'd come back from living at my dad's that I began self-harming. I realise now, years later, that it was attention-seeking. I would arrive late for school and the teachers noticed that I had burns to my hands and arms. I told them I'd done it accidentally, but I hadn't. I was burning myself with matches and lighters. I know Social Services were called about it. I told them the same – that it was an accident. I was behaving quite strangely.

I was again missing my dad. I had no idea where he was living. He had told me he was moving away, but where he'd gone? I didn't have a clue. I would write his name 'Jeff' all over the place, everywhere. I would scratch his name with stones on the footpath and on the walls of houses, I was obsessed. I also started cutting and scratching his name into my arms. I'd use needles that were stuck in the walls, even nails - filthy old nails.

I missed my dad so much, and no matter how much my mum said about him and the bad times they'd had together, I didn't believe it or care. To me my dad was my hero and I had put him on a pedestal. He had gone and I needed him. To me Mark was the villain. He had taken my dad's place and also taken my mum away from me and I resented this. There was many a time when I'd fallen out with Mark that I would say things like, 'I'm going to get my dad to batter you'. I'd say these things even though I hadn't a clue where my dad was.

And I would go into my bedroom and just bang the back of my head against the wall. I used to bite myself and pull my hair out. I was fairly young when I started doing these things, but it got gradually worse as I got older. It just seemed to ease the pressure. I felt that I had nobody to talk to; I just wanted my dad back.

The Social Services thought I was quite a pleasant little girl. I would have preferred to have talked to them away from my mum, but we were all together in one room. I was about nine or ten by this time. It was 1987. My brother was still at home. He was being extremely naughty. He was later taken into care, and many a time I'd hoped I would be taken in care too; I just wanted someone to look after me.

I remember one day the lady from the Social Services had seen me walking home from the supermarket. This was up where the new Tesco store is now. I was loaded up with bags of shopping and I know she wasn't very impressed.

By this time my playing out days had gone. As well as me and Milton, mum had had another baby with Mark, so now I had to look after my little brother Milton and my stepsister Chloe a lot of the time. I was stuck in the house more than ever now. My mum was out at work, my little sister was at the childminder's and I had to get up in the morning, make the beds, do the dishes, hoover and clean the house, then get Milton, my young brother, ready for school. It felt like I was the house slave – a proper little Cinderella!

I had to make up Milton's dinner for the day and there were times when I had to send him off with just a slice of bread in his lunchbox. This was the case on more than one occasion and it wasn't too long before school picked up on it, and the social worker got involved.

But every day was the same. It was always down to me. I was doing the jobs in the house, feeding my brother with whatever there was and on top of that, I was going up to the supermarket twice a week on my own.

It was the same at night. I had to help my mum with the housework after she came home from work. There was a rule whereby, once everything was done, I'd done the dishes and got my baby sister to sleep, I could go out to play, but I could only play out between 6 and 8 o'clock, so if I hadn't got her to sleep by 6 o'clock I couldn't go out. I even used to try to scare her so she would close her eyes. I'd say things like, 'There's a man coming into the room to get you!' and she would close her eyes, hide under the covers and I used to hope she would fall asleep. How cruel was I? But I was that desperate to go out to play.

It was around this time that Milton was being really naughty and was doing all sorts of bad things around the house, like digging the plaster out of the walls and lots of other things. At first they would give him old record players and radios to smash up in the hope that it might stop him destroying the house, but that didn't work.

Social Services decided that he needed to be taken into care. It was a combination of mum not being able to cope with him and because he had become so naughty and disruptive. I think this was because Chloe had been born and was getting all the attention, and like me he was beginning to feel very left out of things.

Being a small child he couldn't understand why all of a sudden he was being pushed to one side and our baby half-sister was getting all the attention. Our situation at home wasn't improving either. There was never any decent food in the house for me to give to Milton for his school lunches.

The social workers had picked up on this and when they came to see Mum and she told them about his naughtiness and how she was finding it difficult to cope, they made the decision to take him into care. He was placed in a children's home and I didn't see him for many weeks. I missed him like mad; he was the only real connection I had left to my dad, but after a while they began to let him come home at the weekends, and at first it was great to see him.

Then that changed for me, because he was coming home in new clothes and with good toys to play with. He would tell me how good the food was and how well he was looked after. He wanted for nothing!

Life for me was as hard as ever and in some respects it became worse. I hardly had any clothes, only one pair of knickers and a couple of pairs of socks, and when I became old enough and I started my first period Mark thought it was funny and made a big joke of it saying things like, 'Hey, here she is, let's get the red flags out!' At first mum bought me proper sanitary towels, but then that stopped and there were times when I literally had to use one of my socks for a towel and wash it through at night so I could use it again the morning after. Mark knew about this, and although there was always money for his precious Chloe for sweets, or for whatever the latest gadget was that he wanted; there was never any money for me even for my sanitary needs.

My joy at seeing my little brother when he came home for those weekends gradually developed into jealousy. It wasn't Milton's fault, but I was still at home and living like the family skivvy. My half-sister was spoilt and even Milton was being better treated than me, by strangers. Because of his situation everything had suddenly changed for him; he was given the best of everything. I still had to make do.

Even though my mum was working and so was Mark, there was never anything decent to eat, unless it was something that Mark had brought home from the farm he worked on. There were times when there was plenty of money, but Milton and me never saw any of it.

Mark would spend any amount of money on himself. He'd go out and buy nice clothes, the best trainers, and new gadgets, like stereo radios and things like that for himself. He had lots of hobbies that were only short-lived and when he got tired of his 'toys' he would sell them. If my new little sister needed anything, it was bought, no questions asked. But when it came down to Milton and me, there were never any treats or new clothes; we had to manage without.

We very often had to go without gas or electricity, in fact at one point we were without electricity for two years as well as always being short of food. It was only later on when the government brought in a law that stated that any household with children under a certain age could not be without electricity or heating that we finally had proper lighting and a fire.

All the self-harming was just to get attention. I even used to ask my mum if I could go into care like Milton. I always asked her on the sly, never when Mark could hear; I could never say anything in front of him as he had a very short fuse and he would kick off. I didn't really get on with Mark from the start. I felt that he had taken my mum away from me. He had taken her bed, a bed that I'd shared with my mum. Suddenly he'd come in and Mum's attention was all for him. We were very often hungry and cold and I blamed him for all this.

He was a very strict man and there were many occasions when he would leather me for next to nothing. I remember once he had come up to my bedroom and had grabbed hold of me and was giving me what for. I swore at him and told him, 'Fuck off. I'm going to get my dad to come here and he will kick ten lots of shit out of you.'

He shouted down to my mum, 'You'd better get up here or I'm going to kill her!' Mum came up and she gave me another good hiding, then she grabbed me by the hair, dragged me downstairs and threw me out of the front door.

I sat on the step and sobbed, wondering where I was going to go. After a while I got up and walked up the hill. There was an alleyway that went down the back of some houses and led to some garages, and I went round the back of there thinking they would come looking for me, but they didn't. When I talk to my mum about it now she laughs and says she could see me the whole time. There were a few times when I'd pack my own bag, get to the bottom of the stairs and shout 'I'm leaving, I'm going now', and the reply would come back, 'OK, go on then, get lost.' I'd go around the block and then back home again. I really wanted to go into a home. I was nothing more than a babysitter. You expect children to do some chores around the house because we all have to learn, but I was just a skivvy who had to do everything and got nothing in return, yet everyone else in the house was showered with treats. I didn't even have a second pair of knickers or any sanitary wear or a hairbrush; I had nothing. I was never rewarded for anything I did.

I felt totally disregarded. He had his daughter, Chloe, she was spoilt rotten, and she could have anything she wanted. She was only two years old and she was given £1 every day. It was my job to take her to the shop to get her sweets; then I had to bring her back and show him that she'd had the money spent on her, and she would sit there and eat the lot.

I got nothing. I could never ask 'Can I have?' because it would never happen. Milton used to come home at the weekend and it was the same for him - he could have just about anything he asked for.

3

Being Groomed

The only treats I ever got were if I did the odd errand for the neighbours. Mr and Mrs Sharples were always very kind and considerate. They knew what a hard time I had at home. I can remember Mr Sharples always had such a nice garden; his lawn was like a bowling green and ours was like a jungle. He even put up a fence at one time to separate us.

I know that he had complained a few times to my mum and Mark about the mess. They would clean it up, but it wasn't long before it was a mess again. Mark wasn't the gardening type; he would rather mess about with old cars. But all this didn't alter the way that the Sharples were always so kind to me.

Then there was another neighbour who lived nearby, he was a man I only ever knew as Edmund; he was a fairly old man, or so I thought in those days. He was probably approaching sixty when I first got to know him. He had been married, but I never met his first wife, I think she had died some years earlier. He did marry another woman later. She was much younger than him, but she didn't stay around for long.

Anyway, Edmund had this wonderful old dog called Suzy, she was big and fat, a cross between a Labrador and a Collie. She was ginger in colour with flecks of white in her coat and I thought at the time she must have been quite old; this might have been because she was so fat, but she had such a loving nature.

I know I was very upset when I heard that Suzy had died. I went round to Edmund's house as usual one day to collect her for her walk and he told me she'd died. He said she had gone to the park and died and hadn't come back. I couldn't get my head around how a dog could just go to the park and die.

The way our houses were laid out was quite uniform and typical of council houses. There was a footpath that ran underneath everyone's front windows, and then the path sort of went down the side of our house towards where Edmund's house was. He had an outhouse which was by the side of the path. I used to sit on our front door step and wait for Suzy to come around.

Sometimes if she didn't come round, I would go round to Edmund's and sit on the step of his outhouse and wait for her there. Suzy and I were like two soulmates; it was as if she knew I needed a friend, and I knew she liked to be loved too. I used to spend hours with her, she was so sweet. Edmund would come out and talk to me. I thought he was just a nice old man in those early days, and he would say to me, 'You really like my dog, don't you, and isn't she fat?' and he would pay me 50p to take her for a walk, but the walks were never long ones because she was so fat and soon got tired.

Edmund would also ask me to do the odd errand for him and would give me 20p for going. Of course living so close to where we lived he knew all about our family and he knew I was having a hard time of it.

My association with Edmund and Suzy probably started when I was about six or seven years old. When I first got to know him, his granddaughter, who was around my age, used to come to his house and we would play together with Suzy, but she stopped coming after a while. As the years went on, and even after Suzy had died and his second wife had left, I still did errands for Edmund.

As I got older and I'd moved to high school I still used to run the odd errand for him. By now he was working nights and sometimes he would pass me when I was going to school in the mornings. Once or twice he would turn the car round and offer to give me a lift to school. I often accepted, especially if it was raining. I lived about two miles from school and I never had any decent clothes to keep the rain out.

He also knew that I smoked – I was only about eleven or twelve. He used to give me the odd cigarette and say he could keep a secret; he wouldn't tell my mum.

At first I didn't catch on, but he would watch for me sometimes and ask me to go to the shops for him and then invite me into his house and offer me cigarettes, promising not to tell anyone. He would let me smoke them in his house and I would sit on his sofa and he would come and sit down next to me and he'd rub my leg, telling me not to worry. He used to joke about it and say it was a game.

I even babysat for his second wife's child a time or two, and I used to hope that she wouldn't go straight to bed when they came in, because he would sit me down and give me cigarettes and offer me drink. Then he would touch me and sometimes it was more than just my leg, but although I didn't like him doing it, I still didn't say anything to anyone. I think I was probably only about eleven then.

He also used to give me money to buy cigarettes, and being a kid and never having had anything I thought this was great. Even when his attentions got more serious and his hands wandered further, I still didn't say anything to my mum. I knew that if I did, I'd probably get the blame.

I don't remember Edmund ever trying to touch me when I was very little. I'd had genuine supportive attention from my neighbours before so I hadn't thought anything of it then, but looking back I do think Edmund was trying to reel me in even then; 'grooming' is the word, by the attention he gave me, the bits of spending money, the dog and having his granddaughter to play with.

He even used to offer to buy me clothes. I would look at a catalogue he had in his house and if I saw something I liked he would make promises to buy it for me. I just thought he was being friendly, but I can't recall him ever touching me then. Not when I was very small. I used to think he was a nice old man.

It was only later that it started, after I'd started at high school and after he'd got me used to having my own money and cigarettes. I suppose I became reliant on him and the gifts he gave me. He would promise me all kinds of things and say that it was our secret. It was around then that things began to get far more serious. I have no idea why he changed. Whether it was something in his make-up or me growing up and him being lonely, I really don't know. Maybe he was just a dirty old man and I was an easy, vulnerable target.

I even used to go and knock on his door in the hope that I'd get something from him or because I needed money for cigarettes. When you're a young girl who has nothing and someone comes along and gives you virtually anything you ask for, and makes promises of even richer gifts, it is very hard to say no.

By this time my involvement with drugs was beginning to have a bit of a hold on me too. I was starting to become dependent on them, using them as a crutch to block out all the bad stuff that was going on in my life, and to help me get through the massive workload I had to cope with at home, as well as school. Thanks to Edmund giving me money I could occasionally afford what I needed.

Things came to a head with Edmund one day. It was a lovely hot summer's afternoon and I was walking home from school. Edmund must have been watching for me through his front door. The door was half-open and he waved to me to go to his house. When I got there he was sitting on the stairs which were facing the front door. He had taken his shirt off and he had his bits out, playing with himself.

He told me to come inside and close the door. He said if I would go upstairs with him and do things to him, he would give me £20. That amount of money to a young girl of only eleven or twelve seemed like winning the lottery in those days, and I was desperate – I was a mess! I followed him upstairs and into his bedroom. He stripped off and wanted me to do stuff to him. I don't know what happened, but I suddenly snapped out of it. Something inside me said 'No.'

'No, I can't do this', I said. I ran downstairs and out of the house. It was horrible! Again I didn't tell my mum, and I suppose like many kids in that situation you blame yourself. You're also afraid that no one will believe you. So you say nothing. You just bottle it all up, put it to the back of your mind and allow it to fester.

Even after that Edmund would still call to me to go to his house, but I wouldn't go near. I had started to go out with a boy when I was about twelve and a half and he would see me coming home with my boyfriend, and he would stare at me. I found him to be so creepy, but I think he must have got the message, and he must have also realised that he had a lot to lose if I ever said what he'd been up to with me. He put his house up for let and moved away.

I did see him some years later. I was driving my car one day and spotted him. I felt like running him down for what he'd done to me. The feeling of utter revulsion that went through me was awful.

I'd heard he had passed the house on to his son. It is only in recent years that I actually told my mum what happened. She said, 'I had a bloody idea something was going on there, why the hell didn't you tell me?'

But I explained to her that at the time I was a rebellious girl and Edmund was giving me things I needed and would let me do things that she wouldn't, like smoking in his house. In a way I was allowing these things to happen out of sheer desperation and he knew that.

But even if I had told her, I don't think she would have believed me at the time. The last time I saw Edmund, I was in a cafe and I saw him walking towards me. I cringed, kept my head down and ran out of the shop. I believe he has since died.

Although Edmund never actually gave me drugs, he was partly responsible for my getting hooked on them at that time. The other person was the dad of a boyfriend – this was a totally different situation though. This guy never attempted to touch me, but he did supply me with the stuff.

I knew his son from living on the estate. His name was Clarke. We were only friends really and I would go round to his house to revise and stuff, and sometimes we'd just sit in his bedroom and natter for ages. The first time I ever tried anything was one night when I'd gone round to their house and my friend was out. I remember I was feeling pretty down with everything that was going on at home and with exams at school, and I suppose the stuff with Edmund was a factor too.

I'd also been offered a job doing a milkround. I already had a job delivering papers and another working on a burger van at the weekends. I was shattered!

My friend's dad picked up on me not being so happy and asked what the matter was. I told him I was having problems and I was constantly tired. I told him I couldn't concentrate on my work at school. He said he had some medication that he took and suggested it might help me. He gave me what looked like two homemade pills and two more to take when I got home. I later learned that it was speed. It was a substance wrapped in a small piece of cigarette paper and I swallowed it with a hot drink.

After that, I was given more pills to help me stay awake, and also became involved in smoking cannabis, but everyone in our crowd was doing this around that time so I can't blame him for that.

Things got so bad though that I ended up not being able to sleep. So he then gave me some Temazapam to help me to sleep. He gave me ten of these in total and one morning, when I'd been awake for a long time and was feeling really strange, I looked at the tablets and thought, take the lot!

I know I took quite a few of these pills before going to school. When I got to school I collapsed in the middle of registration and was taken to the medical room. The teachers knew right away what the problem was and decided to just let me sleep it off all day. But they did take me home later and told my mum what had happened.

Although there was no direct connection between Edmund and my friend's dad, they were both responsible for grooming me in different ways, and for their own perverted reasons. Without Edmund's money, I wouldn't have been able to afford the drugs that my friend's dad had to offer, and he got me hooked so that I would buy more and more from him.

4

Blake

At the age of twelve I was a real tomboy. I would do anything for a laugh and got up to all sorts of mischief. I had loads of friends – boys and girls, all of who lived on our estate. I'd find any excuse to go out to play, often taking my sister out with me. We would hang around mainly on the school playing fields at St Mary's High School. We'd go up there, sit on the grass and watch the lads playing football at the weekend, either Saturday or Sunday.

One particular day there was a new lad who'd joined in. At first I didn't take much notice of him, but he did catch my eye because he had such an amazing smile. He wasn't that tall and he was quite trim with dark hair, blue eyes and he had eyelashes that went on forever.

One day when we were up there watching the lads playing footy, my cousin Lucy turned up. She was going out with one of the other lads who were playing that day and she saw me looking at this lad. He was quite a bit older than me. I was only about twelve and he was around sixteen, but I was really taken by his smile. I happened to say to Lucy, 'He's nice, I fancy him. Isn't he nice?' We were just a couple of young girls giggling their heads off and being silly. I'd found out his name was Blake, but then Lucy just shouted out to him, 'Hey, Jeanette fancies you'. I could have died. My head went down – I was so embarrassed. I said 'Oh, I'm going now'. But after that I would go back every weekend and one day Lucy's boyfriend said to me, 'You fancy him, don't you?' and I said, 'Yeah I do, he's nice.' He said 'I'll ask him out for you' – as lads do! In those days a lad would usually just say something like, 'Will you go out with me?'

Anyway, he did ask him if he fancied going out with me, but he said no; because he already had a girlfriend. That was the story of my life: I was used to getting knock-backs and disappointments in my life, but I just kept going back every week and having a quick look at him.

Then there was a time just before we were due to go on our family holiday to Scarborough. I had gone out sell-ing things for my mum and Mark; it was usually videos and stuff like that. I had called at this house one night and it happened to be the house where he lived, although I didn't know that at the time. A little lady answered the door. She asked me in and had a look at what I was selling. She liked the videos I was selling and bought some and asked me to call again.

I went round again one night taking my videos with me and he answered the door. At the time I just shrugged it off and got on with selling my stuff. When I think back about it now, there I was calling at the house of the lad I fancied. I'd got to know his mum quite well by now and I think I must have told her a bit about myself and how I had to be in for a certain time, and I think she must have talked about me to him, because he seemed to change; he seemed to look at me differently and started to smile at me when he saw me.

One day, near to the time we were due to go on our holiday in August he asked me if I wanted to meet him at the shop at such and such a time. I think he'd found out from his mum that I wasn't allowed out after a set time.

So he said he could meet me at the shops at 8 o'clock. This was right on my deadline. I could only go out after

I'd got my jobs done and my little sister settled, so I had to think of some excuse to get out. It was about five to eight and I shouted to my mum that we had run out of milk. She gave me some money and I ran all the way round to the shops on Royal Avenue. The shops were part of a big building with steps on either side that led up to flats above. It was quite an easy place to hide.

He was already there when I got there and we sat together on the steps and had a natter. We sat near to the bottom because the shops backed on to where our house was and my mum would have been able to see me. He told me the reason he'd said no to going out with me before was because he'd got a girlfriend, but he said he was thinking of dumping her.

He knew I was about to go on holiday and he asked if I wanted to meet him again when I got back and said we could talk about going out together. He came across as being quite shy and a bit nervous. I can remember beaming and thinking 'Yeah, I've got a boyfriend.' And when I left he gave me a kiss. I was really chuffed on the way home, but I wondered afterwards if he'd done it so I wouldn't go off with anyone else while I was away on holiday; if so, he was right – thinking I had now got myself a boyfriend, I had no intention of looking for anybody else!

Our holiday to Scarborough was always a brilliant time. There were so many of us that went. This particular year there must have been about a dozen of us altogether; kids and adults. As well as my mum and Mark, there were my little sister Chloe, my brother Milton, Lucy and her brother Darren, my Uncle Tony (he was really my cousin but I always called him uncle because he was quite a bit older than me) and some friends of mum and Mark.

My stepdad had bought a secondhand caravan which he sold straight after our holiday. It was quite an old one, but it was pretty big and fully functional with a big awning on the side. The adults slept inside and all us kids piled into the awning.

We went to Scarborough most years, always to the same site. It was Scalby Manor, which was just outside Scarborough on the road north towards Whitby. We either stayed in a caravan or sometimes in a trailer-tent that Mark had bought just for the holiday but we always had a fantastic time. There was lots to do on the site and nearby, but one of the things I liked best was the chippy teas – brilliant! There was never any set time to come in, which was great, and because there were so many of us it meant I wasn't tied to looking after Chloe all the time.

We all stayed together as a family until lunchtime and then the adults went back to the caravan and they wanted us out of the way, so off we'd go, getting up to all sorts of mischief. As I said, I was a real tomboy and I loved nothing better than going off round the rock pools collecting cockles and winkles and taking them back for my mum and Mark. I sometimes collected so many that we ended up throwing them away.

Of course I never realised at the time that these things were alive. I just knew that my mum liked eating them and I had seen her eating them at home and never thought anything about it, but one day I saw her trying to get this thing out of the shell with a pin and screamed, 'Oh my God, it's alive!'

Then I realised that I had caught these poor winkles and cockles, and thrown loads of them in the bin, still alive! That was it. I saw this black thing on the end and thought it was an eye; I didn't catch any more after that.

The caravan campsite we were on was in a great place. There was a beach just below our site and to reach it we had to go down some quite steep concrete steps set in the cliffside, but once you were down there it was brilliant. I don't think the tide ever came right in but it was very rocky. Me being the tomboy that I was in those days, I decided I would do the big thing and climb the cliffs to the top. Lucy decided she would climb with me and at first it was OK. It wasn't too steep and it was a bit sandy.

I went first and was quite a way in front of Lucy. I'd got past the sandy part and was on the rocky part and it was getting a bit steep. Lucy slipped on the sandy part below, slipping down to a ledge. She decided she wasn't going any further, and made her way back up the steps. But by this point I couldn't turn back – I couldn't get back down so I carried on to the top. It was all going well until I reached the top, where there was a bit of an overhang and the top was grassy and loose. No matter how I tried I couldn't get a proper grip on anything. Every time I grabbed a handful of grass, it came away in my hand along with lots of soil. By now I was very high up and becoming pretty scared – I couldn't go back down and I couldn't get up. Luckily my cousin Darren was at the top, he'd come along to meet us and he managed to lie flat on the grass. He took hold of my hand and pulled me up.

If he hadn't been there that day, I wouldn't be here now. But that was typical of me – the stupid things you do when you're a child! It was fine to go down but coming back up I'd wanted to climb and so had Lucy. I was full of mischief, a real daredevil, and I would have a go at anything. It was a child's trick, but I never went that way again and I never did tell my mum about that adventure.

Our weeks in Scarborough were wonderful times. We used to love going to Water Splash World, a big open air water park with slides galore, and also to Peasholm Park. The squirrels used to come and take nuts out of your hand. I never had any nuts but I used to pretend I had; then one day somebody got bitten by one of them and I didn't do it again. My stepdad, Mark was chased by the swans and pecked; he never went back to the park after that.

We used to race up and down the steep hills and we also enjoyed going to the fairground at the other end of the bay; even though I never had any money to go on anything I liked watching everything that was going on. I used to go around the harbour watching the men gutting the fish and it stank, but I loved it – I was such a tomboy I should have been a boy!

We also used to climb up the hill to the castle and I can remember seeing an old graveyard and a grave that had someone special in it, I think it was Anne Bronte's. It was someone like that: famous and from the past!

The freedom we had on those holidays was fantastic. We used to walk from our caravan park right round the road to where the fairground was and back again. We just had loads of energy. I couldn't do it now, I'd be shattered! I think that year was best because I had Lucy with me; she hadn't come on other years. And the weather always seemed so good too; it was always warm and sunny.

We were given a couple of pounds a day and we would either spend it on going to Water Splash World or sometimes we'd buy cigarettes with it. We'd sometimes only come in at 10 o'clock at night and the adults would already be asleep inside and us lot would pile into the awning. The things we used to get up to were hilarious. It was great, no stress.

I remember one night, Lucy was being an absolute idiot, she had us in stitches shining her torch and pulling all sorts of weird faces to frighten us. She reached up for another torch that was hanging from the top of the awning and she pulled the awning down on us. We were in stitches. It was all childish play and then Mum shouted out, 'What the bloody hell's going on out there?' And we thought, Oh, Jesus! How are we going to put this back together? Then, still laughing our heads off we tried to sort it out.

Our holiday was fantastic. It was only one week, but we absolutely loved it. All the pressure was off for one week but then it was back home again. The journey was always a hard one, because there were so many of us and

all the luggage too. We all had to be distributed into different people's cars. I know Tony didn't drive and neither did
Sally, but Robert did. We even had people in the caravan
at one point. I don't think the police stopped you then, like
they do now.

It was just one week a year and we used to go out and
sell what we could to have that holiday. I know caravan
holidays are cheap, but Mark always had to have plenty
of money in his pocket to go and spend, and that is what
they'd do all day, do their thing. I know we were given
some money and we had our fish and chips, but for that
one week I didn't have care in the world – apart from
hanging off a cliff!

Once back home it wasn't long before I saw Blake
again. I'd gone down to the shop for my mum and there
he was. I hadn't arranged to meet him, it just happened.

'Oh, you're back. Do you fancy coming round to my
house later, about half past six?' he asked.

'OK', I said.

It was from there that our relationship developed and
I became his girlfriend. Although I'd had lots of boys as
friends, I'd never had a serious boyfriend in that sense
before.

I went round and that night we just watched telly. I
hadn't told him that I could only be out between six and
eight, but I think he grasped that. I think his mum might
have told him. Watching TV was never something that ap-
pealed to me, it never has and it still doesn't today. We
never had a telly at home until later on. You might have
thought it was something that I'd have wanted, but it did
nothing for me and it still doesn't. Music was what I liked;
and I still do!   .

Blake had a record player in his room. I remember he
had an old LP. I think it was called 'All Woman'. I was into
female singers such as Gloria Gaynor and Aretha Franklin
and there was a track on it called 'Piano in the dark'. I used

to play that track over and over again.

I was thirteen years old by now, and I used to meet Blake whenever I could get out of the house. Of course, I had to have my jobs done and make sure my little sister was asleep. I hadn't told my mum at this point that I was seeing a lad, but Blake's mum and dad were fine with me. I thought they were quite nice people. His mum was called Angie, she was a short, but rather large lady who worked really hard. She had something like three jobs on the go and she wasn't all that well.

Because she was such a big lady she soon became very tired and used to rest in between jobs. She would come home from one job in the morning and have a nap before going to her next job in the afternoon and the same again before her evening job. She must have been shattered! She was always working, mainly cleaning which is a very strenuous job and she never really looked well. It must have taken it out of her. She was a very quiet lady, but one who spoke her mind if she had anything to say.

Blake's stepdad, Bradley was an old-fashioned type of guy, quite fit. He looked much younger than he actually was, but he smoked like a factory chimney ... at least 100 cigarettes a day. He would light one after another. The living room in their house resembled an opium den. He worked for a removal company, so I think there was a fair bit of money coming in; they also seemed to have quite a bit of debt, but it was a manageable sort of debt.

I can remember people coming to the door, people like the Provident man and others would call for money, but they were always out at the weekends – Friday, Saturday and Sunday, enjoying themselves, drinking and getting drunk.

Blake's two younger brothers, Patrick and Karl didn't get on too well with Bradley. He was their stepfather not their real dad. He was pretty stern with them, they fought a lot and he would chase them and curse them when they wouldn't behave. He'd shout at them and tell them, 'Get up them bloody stairs' and they'd call him names too and tell him to get lost. They still wanted their own dad, even though he was quite a violent man they still loved him and seemed to resent Brad. They did still see their own dad, and I suppose they wanted him there in a way, and not Brad. They couldn't understand at that age.

I thought they were really funny little lads. They went to the same school as I did and if they saw me they would come running up the road to me, their schoolbags hanging down their backs, and because they were such short kids their bags hung so low that they banged their legs as they ran. They used to tell everybody, 'She's going out with my brother'. They were really cute little lads.

The early days with Blake were good. Most evenings when I was allowed out to play I went round to his house and I could see him waiting for me; he would be at his window watching for me if I was a little bit late. It all depended on if I could get my sister to sleep, but to see him looking for me made me feel wanted. It felt good knowing that someone cared. We would go to his room and talk about what had happened that day and how things were at home. I explained about not being allowed out until my jobs were done and he accepted that, but he did think it was cruel and horrible. He was good to me in those days, I had been a smoker for a while by this time and he would give me cigarettes; he was working and could afford them.

He always used to say that he would never hit me because that was something that his dad had done to his mum and he thought it was awful. So I remember feeling that I had got someone who was truthful to me and who wouldn't harm me in any way at all, so it made me feel as if it was going to be a nice longlasting relationship, and that he was a good person.

Because of that I allowed him to become close and opened up to him. I had always created barriers before. I suppose I felt loved and safe because I thought I was with someone who cared. He'd said those words to me and it made me feel good as well as safe with him.

Blake wasn't my first 'boyfriend', but he was my first serious boyfriend. I'd had lots of lads who I called my friends and lots that I'd been out with, as you do at that age, but none of them had come close to being anything like serious. For a long time our relationship was just boyfriend and girlfriend, and it took quite a long while before it became a sexual thing. We would lie on his bed listening to music and we'd kiss and cuddle and there was a bit of petting but that was as far as it went.

The sexual side of the relationship began later, although I was still only about thirteen and a half. Blake was my first boyfriend in that way. I remember it was one night that his mum and dad had gone out and left us alone in the house. We were in his room and he decided he was going to go downstairs and get some drink. His stepdad nearly always had stash of booze of one kind or another in the house.

He came back up and offered me some, and I decided I would have a drink too. I think that sort of relaxed me and gave me the confidence to do what came next. As the night wore on, one thing led to another and that was that. But when you've done it once it sort of becomes a regular thing after that. It seems to be the first thing you do when you walk through the door.

5

Pregnant - at just fifteen

By this time my mum knew I was seeing Blake, but I still
had to be in for 8 o'clock. I was still not fourteen yet and
although I knew a bit about the facts of life, I had never
for one moment thought about contraception. It wasn't
something we'd ever talked about at home and I'd never
done sex education at school either.

My mum had said, 'Don't you dare get pregnant', but
she never once sat me down and talked to me seriously
about the risks or anything like that, and I suppose in a
way, I didn't care anyway. I can remember thinking, what
if I did get pregnant – I knew I might, but when we had
started having regular sex, it never it was never an issue
that maybe I should have some sort of contraception.

But as I became sexually more active, I can remember
thinking, Oh Jesus, I could get pregnant but I shrugged
it off and thought Oh well, whatever! It was obvious to
anyone that if you carry on like that sooner or later the
inevitable is going to happen, and of course, it did!

At the time I found out that I was pregnant, I was only
fourteen and a half and at first I wouldn't accept that it
was happening to me. This particular day, I was at home.
It was early morning, I was up and dressed and ready for
school and I started to be sick. It happened so quickly that
I had to grab the living room bin to be sick into. I was sick

all the way to school, and even though I knew you got pregnant by doing what Blake and me had been doing, I still couldn't accept that it might be happening to me. My mum looked at me and said, 'You had better not be pregnant, girl!'

I said, 'You are joking, aren't you? I've not had sex – I'm not pregnant!' – as you do.

She knew I was seeing Blake, he was coming round to our house by this time and they had accepted him, but even so the rules were still just as strict about the time I had to be in. If ever I was one minute past eight I got battered, and although they knew I was with Blake, they seemed to make it an even bigger issue than ever.

I know there was one particular night when Blake had walked me home, I was so embarrassed. We were out at the front and it was actually raining at the time and I stayed there at the front door chatting to him for a while and I thought, It'll be all right, they can see I'm here, they know I'm home, but once I walked through the door I got a real good hiding. The worst part of it was, Blake was still at the door talking to my mum, but Mark got hold of me and gave me what for.

A couple of days after I'd had the sickness my mum had got me in to see the nurse. I remember sitting in the waiting area of the surgery at Balfour Court, Central Park Surgery. I was sure everything was going to be fine – I was convinced there was no way this would happen to me, it was the sort of thing that happened to other girls, not me.

My mum said to me, 'What if you are, what are you going to do?' and I replied, 'I won't be, I'll prove you wrong'.

The next thing the nurse came in and confirmed it and mum went mad, shouting at me, 'Now what are you going to do?'

I just said 'I don't know' and she said it was all down to me and that I should know. But I was only a kid. What did I know about being pregnant and stuff like that?

That night Blake came round, and mum had made sure Mark was going to be out. She told Blake that I was pregnant and asked him what he was going to do about it.

'Well we'll just have to make the best of it, we'll have to manage', he said.

'Are you going to stick around then?' she asked him, and he said, 'Yes, of course I am.'

My mum told Mark about it all and he flipped. She made sure she told him when I was out of the house. He didn't speak to me for months after that. He wouldn't even look at me. My mum's concern was how we were going to manage; it meant another mouth to feed and on top of that, I was still at school. She still wasn't convinced that Blake would stick around. He had said he would, but that didn't necessarily mean he meant it, and she was worried.

So was I for that matter, especially later on in the pregnancy, because I had become so big. I had stretch marks everywhere and everyone had said to me he would leave me. I believed them and I was frightened that he would, because I thought, Who the hell is going to want me, looking like this? It seemed to be everyone's perception that he wouldn't stick around.

My mum spoke to the school and Social Services as well. They wanted me to continue with my school work up to and even after I'd had the baby. They suggested my mum could mind the child while I carried on with my education. But the kids at school were horrible to me, even worse than before. They looked at me as if I was carrying a disease; it wasn't normal for a young girl of my age to be pregnant and they made life very hard for me.

I had always found it hard at school. It wasn't too bad just after I came back from living with my dad, but things got worse later, once the decent clothes began to get tatty and I was dubbed 'The Tramp' again. I would often go and hide in the school toilets at breaktime. They were cold and horrible, big brick buildings that were set away from the school. There was no plaster on the walls and what paint there was, was peeling off. They were cold and damp, and they stank of pee, and worse, but I would rather be in there than taking all the flak from the other kids.

It came to a head when it was time for me to take my exams. The teachers offered to get me a special chair to sit in so that I'd be comfortable, and they did, but all the kids were looking at me and sniggering and saying things – that was it; I walked out there and then and didn't complete my exams. I left school at fifteen because the kids were just so cruel. I had tried, but it was no good. My time after that was spent helping my mum with her job, which was to pack cards into envelopes; I did this mainly just to pass the time.

My mum's family were also a bit funny with me until after Hayley had been born and then they came round. Most of the neighbours were OK, especially Mr and Mrs Sharples next door. I could never do anything wrong in their eyes, they were brilliant with me.

Blake had it even worse than me. When he told his mum and dad what had happened, he had a big falling out with them and they kicked him out. He had always told them there was nothing going on between us, but when they learned the truth and knowing how old I was, his mum kicked him out.

He came round to our house and my mum ended up putting him up with us. Obviously, we weren't allowed to stay in the same room, but mum thought it was a good thing him being with us, because if I went into labour, he was there. Surprisingly Mark wasn't bothered, I think he was quite happy because Blake had a job and was giving him money towards his keep and he was also giving them money for my keep as well.

He was working for a company on Moss Side in Leyland. I think they used to pack car parts and stuff like that. It wasn't something he talked about much and I didn't really ask; he considered himself to be the breadwinner and as far as he was concerned that's all I needed to know.

The strange thing was that because we were living under the same roof, I didn't have to go out and the 8 o'clock curfew wasn't an issue any more, but that wasn't such a good thing, because it meant I never got out at all and we didn't seem to have any time together any more. As a result we started fighting. Until then he hadn't really been violent towards me. He had once slapped me around the face when we were in his bedroom, but he was very upset about it and promised me nothing like that would ever happen again, but it did.

I suppose living under the same roof didn't help the situation, as we started to get on one another's nerves. The only time we had a break from each other was when Blake was at work. The first time it got really nasty was while I was still pregnant. It must have been around July or August because my mum and Mark had gone away on holiday like they always did in the summer. They left Blake and I on our own and I must have said something to upset him and he threw a full can of Coke at my head.

We were fighting when my cousin Tony came in; he hadn't gone with them on holiday that particular year. My mum had asked him to keep his eye on us and he caught us fighting and Blake hitting me. He said he was going to tell my mum and I begged him not to, I pleaded because mum would throw Blake out if she found out.

Around that time we had applied for a council house of our own, but because I was so young it had to be Blake who applied, as he was 18 and working. By the time mum and Mark got back from holiday the council had said there was a house nearby that was ready to move into, but the rules then were much stricter and they said my mum would have to sign on my behalf. My mum said no at that particular time because she thought I was still too young, even though I was pregnant.

So we stayed living at my house right through the pregnancy. My mum had a hard time with me. I had a massive craving for beef flavoured Hula Hoops and I would eat as many as ten packets a day. My poor mum used to trail from shop to shop trying to buy these things for me. She would go down to our local shop and they were always selling out of them just because I ate so many of them. One of the reasons I wanted so many was because although I wasn't usually a big eater, people told me I had to eat for two now and I took this literally. The Hula Hoops were just about the only food I could tolerate as most things made me feel sick.

This didn't help with the way I looked either. I was huge, and now covered in stretch marks. I was scared of losing Blake and being left on my own with a baby. I think I must have thought about my mum's situation when my dad left and I didn't want that for my baby. I felt very insecure; I needed someone to look after me.

I was very immature though, and Social Services did get on my case. I do remember one woman coming round who was a health visitor and she would feel my belly to see how high I was. I don't remember anyone else ever doing that since. I can't remember her name, but I was quite lippy with her, giving her lots of backchat, and she said to me, 'I'm going to be watching you like a hawk, young lady, and if I get one inkling that you're not going to look after this baby, it will be taken off you.' I think it was because of my immaturity and because I gave my mum so much trouble. I thought to myself, Oh shit! I knew I had to start growing up.

6

Hayley

I went into labour in the early hours of 11th October 1993 and was taken into Sharoe Green hospital in Preston at 5 o'clock in the morning. I had no idea what to expect and it was a bloody big shock to me once the labour started. Blake was there, but he just wasn't what I'd hoped he would be. He didn't seem supportive at all, he just sat there as if to say 'C'mon, bloody hurry up' and he showed no interest at all. He never asked if I was all right or encouraged me by saying 'You're doing OK, you'll be all right', there was just nothing coming from him.

My mum was more supportive than he was and I was as ratty as anything with all the pain. I had been in labour for nine and a half hours before they decided I needed an emergency caesarean. Everyone was rushing around. It was quite scary for a young girl like me. One minute someone is coming in and shaving your bits down there. I thought, Whoa! Hold on a minute. What the hell's going on?

Then a young nurse came in to check how dilated I was and my waters broke. She was very apologetic. But next minute Hayley's foot was showing and they realised then that I would have to have an emergency section. The baby was being born in the breech position.

Hayley was eventually born very quickly after getting into theatre. As soon as she was born I cried. She weighed

7lb 13oz and had a load of black hair. I remember thinking how gorgeous she looked. They took her straight down to the ward afterwards. We had chosen the name Hayley, after the actress Hayley Mills. Mark had been going on about her and I think I went along with that to please him as much as anything.

We stayed at Sharoe Green for the first couple of days and then they transferred us to Chorley Hospital. It was much better at Chorley. Sharoe Green was OK, but it was so busy. It was as if no one had any time to help you with anything. Chorley was far better. It was a much more relaxed place and the nurses showed me all sorts.

I remember I had lots of presents brought in for Hayley like little clothes and I would spend hours changing her and trying all these nice new things on her. I think the hospital must have picked up on this and said something to Social Services, because their attitude towards me had changed so much once I got home.

Another good point about Chorley Hospital was that there was a day room right by the side of my ward and I could nip out for a cigarette, knowing I didn't have to go far and leave Hayley for long.

Obviously our lives changed dramatically from that day, because I was now a mum and Blake was a dad, but I was even more scared that he would leave. I can remember ringing him from hospital the day after I'd given birth – I had to ring Mr Sharples' phone because my mum didn't have a phone in those days and mobiles weren't around like they are today. Blake came to the phone and I remember crying and saying, 'I want to come home, I just want to come home.'

He told me there was no way I could come home. He said I had to stay in hospital for ten days because I'd had an emergency section. I told him there was no way I was staying in hospital for ten days.

I eventually did come home after seven days. All the thoughts and worries that I'd had about Blake leaving or playing away were confirmed then. He'd been missing from home for two days. It turned out he'd been staying at his ex-girlfriend's house.

But with having a baby to look after, and the fact that he was financially supporting us, I just had to kind of deal with it, although it was awful. He then got me into a position where he could do what he wanted, and I had to do what he said, and there was nothing I could do about it.

I was living under my mum's roof and although my mum was very supportive with me and helped a lot with Hayley, I hated it there. I'd got a new baby, and I wanted out; I wanted a place of my own. My next thing I wanted was a house. We'd lived with my mum for ages by now; it was finally around August and Hayley was ten months old, when my mum accepted I could go.

It was more of a priority if you had a baby when it came to getting a council house and because we had and were living with my mum, we were offered a house on another avenue, still on our estate, and just around the corner from my mum's. When we moved in we had very little furniture. We were given a grant of £200 to help us and we got a cooker and a fridge and one or two other bits with the money.

We were given an old brown settee by a woman a couple of doors away and we had a threadbare carpet that had been left in the house. It was the only carpet in the house. We couldn't afford anything. We even had an old sheet hung up at the window for a curtain. If Blake hadn't spent all his money going out drinking we would have been all right, but I could never have said that to him. When I look back, I can't believe I lived like that.

It was a complete learning curve for me. I had to learn how to become a housewife, mother and a cook, and I had to learn quickly. We'd only been in our new house for about a week when I nearly burned the place down. I had put the chip pan on to get hot, ready to cook the tea and had gone out of the room doing something else. When I went back to it there were flames all over the top of the fat and round the pan.I grabbed a wet cloth out of the sink and threw it onto the pan but the whole thing went up. There was fat and flames everywhere. I just panicked and grabbed Hayley and ran outside shouting and screaming. The fire brigade came and soon had everything under control. Luckily there wasn't too much damage done and even luckier for me, Blake arrived home while the fire brigade were still there.

He couldn't very well have a go at me with them there, and he could see I was in shock. I remember thinking at the time, Oh hell, we haven't got much and it's all going up in smoke!

I was only sixteen and having a baby and a house to run at that age is a big worry, and I was worried. I was also quite excited, but scared all the same. I was worried about money and Blake wasn't the sort of man who would readily hand over his wages even though he was on quite a good wage and I was receiving family credits. I still found it very hard to manage and I was up in court at one point for not having paid my council tax, or Poll Tax as it was then, but I didn't think I should have paid it because I wasn't even eighteen at the time. I never told Blake about that as he would have gone mad.

He had by this time changed his job. He was now working as a landscape gardener for a small local firm. Blake took to Hayley like a duck to water; he doted on her and she could do no wrong. It was like that all the time. He let her get away with murder. The only time he was ever nasty with her was much later on. It was one night when he was drunk and she woke up crying and keeping him awake. He went in to her and I thought he was going to kill her. He pushed her face right into the pillow to shut her up, telling her, 'Shut up you little bitch or I'll effing well kill you.' Before that, and even after, he would always feel really guilty if he so much as slapped her leg. In a way, he behaved with her how my dad had always been with me.

He always wanted to go out drinking on Friday, Saturday and Sunday like his mum and stepdad did, so his wages were blown on that. It took a hell of a chunk of his wages. He used to go up to the Cricket Club on Fox Lane and meet his dad there. His dad was always giving his kids such a lot of grief that when Blake came home he would be in a vile temper.

There was one night when he'd come back from an afternoon with his dad and he absolutely battered me. I told my mum that I'd fallen between the bikes that were kept in our hallway, but that wasn't true, he had given me a right good hiding. How my nose is as nice and straight as it is today, I will never know.

I remember looking in the mirror and thinking, Jesus Christ! My teeth were covered in blood, I had two black eyes and my nose was busted open. I had big footprints all over my ribcage where he had taken a run and jumped on me when I was on the settee.

He could easily have killed me, I was only little, but the thing was, I just accepted it and I think it was because I didn't want to go back home to my mum's house. The fights got more and more frequent because he still carried on going out drinking with his dad. He was a totally different person from when he lived at home with his mum. He wasn't violent then.

The violence had become a regular thing and why I put up with it I'll never know. I suppose I thought I loved him, and it became a way of life. I was hit when he was sober and even more when he'd been drinking. He was often full of remorse the next day when he'd sobered up and sometimes he would cry and sob like a baby saying he was sorry, and of course, like a fool, I believed him.

I became programmed in a certain way. I had a routine and I knew I had to have everything just so or he would lose it with me. He liked his meals ready and on the table when he walked through the door. The house had to be clean and his clothes washed and ready for him. I would go around the house time after time just checking that I'd done everything. I was walking on eggshells the whole time.

Then one day he came home and said he'd decided he was going to join the army. It had been something he had always considered, but until now he hadn't done anything about it. I suppose the time must have felt right to him. The military life was in his blood. All his family had been in the services in one form or another, and I think he saw it as a natural progression.

He was now getting on better with his mum and dad because of Hayley, and they had always wanted him to go into the army so the time seemed right; and he thought that it might give us all a better way of life. A better area and more money, as well as providing him with a career, and as much as I liked the idea I was still afraid because it meant us moving away, and all through his training I was worried he might not come back.

The first thing he had to do was to go to Preston to the Army Careers Office to see about enrolling. Within a week of doing this they had sent him over to Catterick in Yorkshire. He spent the day there doing various tests – such as aptitude and fitness, and he had to have a medical. He passed them all. I was a bit surprised at that because he was quite a porky bloke and didn't come across as being all that fit at the time, even though he thought he was God's gift in some ways.

In one way I was hoping he wouldn't have passed; I didn't really want to move away. I suppose I felt some level of safety in being near to my family, even though I was still getting beaten up all the time, and I was worried that life could get worse if I didn't have that safety net.

Six weeks after his day at Catterick he was called back

for an interview. It wasn't long after that that he got a letter telling him he was going to Pirbright in Surrey to do his training, he first had to collect his ticket from a certain address and it also told him when his first pay would be paid into his bank account. His regiment was to be the 1st Royal Green Jackets.

I was also worried that if he did decide to go off and leave me for his new life then I would be all alone, a single mum covered in stretch marks from head to toe and who would ever want me looking like that? On top of all that, I knew I couldn't trust him where other girls were concerned and it was always at the back of my mind that he would have affairs.

Anyway, off he went to join the army and do his initial training. His initial training at Pirbright was to last for ten or twelve weeks, during which time he would have a break and come home for two weeks.

At the time I was still living in our own house with Hayley, but being on my own and having all the worry of him being away and having very little money drove me to despair. I was still paying off the fine I had for the Poll Tax bill and I just couldn't cope any more, so I decided to try to kill myself.

I went traipsing around all the shops in town buying packets of Anadin Extra. I remember the shops would only sell you so many at a time, because of the dangers of taking them, so I had to go to different shops to make sure I had enough to do the job. I also bought a bottle of Strawberry Ribena and there I was walking home taking one tablet and having a drink of this awful Strawberry Ribena, then another tablet and another drink. I hadn't been home long before I realised the significance of what I'd done and I called my next door neighbour, Mrs Branto, and told her I'd tried to kill myself.

'What? You stupid little thing', she said, and straight away called my mum, who also gave me a hell of an earbashing. I was taken to hospital and had my stomach pumped with some awful charcoal stuff.

After that my mum insisted I move back in with her. I didn't want to, but I did. The time at home was OK for a while, but then Mum and I started arguing because I wasn't being allowed out. My mum would say things like, 'No, you're not going out; you have a baby now and can't just please yourself.' I felt like a prisoner and hated it. I had to find a way of getting out of there.

About five weeks into Blake's training, he came home on leave for two weeks. I was surprised to see him when he walked up the path, but I can remember thinking, Oh, you have come back? During his time at home we discussed Hayley and me moving down there; it was what we all wanted and with things not being too good at home, I decided to do something about it.

I had been in touch with the Army Family Liaison Office to see about us moving down south to be nearer Blake. It wasn't long after he'd gone back to resume his training that I got a letter to say they had found accommodation for Hayley and myself at a place called the Cotswold Centre, which was a centre for homeless army families in Corsham, Wiltshire. It was only temporary accommodation – a sort of transit camp until somewhere more permanent could be found for us.

After Blake had completed his basic training at Pirbright, he had to go to Aldershot to do his trade training. He was to train to be a chef. It was while he was at Aldershot that I had a problem with some nodules on my womb and I needed to have a small operation. I was really struggling for money and I was quite upset about it. The staff at the hospital asked where my husband was and why he wasn't coming to see me. I told them he was doing his trade training and that he couldn't get time off. They said that was rubbish. They rang him up and gave him a right bollocking. He came home that weekend and took it out of me. I'd made his tea but he thought it wasn't hot enough, so he threw the plate against the wall, and forced me down onto the floor, making me eat the food from the broken pieces of crockery. Then he laid into me, still fuming with rage; he was kicking and beating me. The guards who were on duty patrolling the quarters heard him and luckily for me, they came rushing in to stop him. All his anger was because he'd had to come back to Corsham to see me.

7

Getting married

I hadn't been down at Corsham for long when out of the blue we decided it was about time we got married. Because I wasn't getting on too well with my mum, it was left to Blake's mum to make the arrangements. She was brilliant but I hadn't even been expecting my mum to agree to come.

Then one day, Angie, Brad, my mum and Mark turned up at our place. Angie had managed to talk my mum round, and we made our peace. But most of the arrangements had already been made by this time by Angie. She had bought my dress from a woman who was advertising it in the paper for £50. She had booked the Navy Club in town, they were members there and they got the room for free. They also knew a guy who ran a mobile disco and he did it for free. Angie made Hayley's dress and she also made the entire buffet. It was all done on a tight budget. All in all it cost about £650.

I happened to know a guy who had a car showroom in town and he lent us a car to take me to the registry office and then to the reception. It was actually a Lamborghini; a very classy motor!

We had decided we were getting married on Saturday 27th January 1996. We travelled up from Corsham on the Friday. Blake had some stupid ideas about the way we should do things. He decided he should stay at his mum and dad's and I should stay at mine on the night before our wedding day. I thought this was a stupid idea especially as he said he wanted to meet me at the park that night and then walk me home to my mum's house.

We had about thirty guests, which included Mr and Mrs Sharples. Our witnesses were all friends of his from the army. The wedding day itself went really fast and the honeymoon was nonexistent. Blake said he had to go straight back the following morning, he told me he had to be on some army exercise or other, so the following morning (Sunday) he was up at six o'clock and caught the early morning train back to camp. I stayed on and went back on the Monday.

It wasn't until much later that I learnt that anyone getting married is excused any kind of duties and is allowed two weeks off. I must have been very gullible, I thought later. He was probably off with his mates somewhere in Amsterdam having his own little honeymoon. He had never been loyal to me and looking back it was more of a marriage of convenience.

Around this time Blake finished his basic training and started his trade training. I decided to stay on in the Cotswolds until Blake had finished his trade training. The homes we were in were mainly full of women. Blake was away during the week doing his training and came home at the weekends. Because it was nearly all women living there on their own we had guards patrolling around the accommodation at night, so it was very secure.

Blake was now well into his trade training, only coming home at the weekends, and there were some weekends when he just didn't bother coming home. One particular weekend he had come home, dropped off his bag and gone out. I decided to empty his bag and started to get his chef's whites out for washing.

As I was sorting everything out, a letter and a photograph

fell out. The photograph was of a young blonde girl who was completely nude. The letter said she couldn't wait until they were together and she could be a mother to my Hayley. She had sprayed the letter with perfume and signed it Anna. I flipped – I sat there fuming and waited for him to come home.

When he came in I had it out with him, and strangely enough he didn't fight with me, which I was expecting him to. He was more shocked that I'd found out. He was angry that I'd gone into his bag, but I had only done that to get his whites out for washing. It turned out this girl was on the same course as him.

I told him I was going to see the families' officer and I did. The families' officer came round to see him and it turned out the girl was only sixteen and was what was known as a 'Boy Soldier'. She had only just qualified to go in and was only there during termtime to do her training. Her service couldn't start until she turned eighteen. She was training to be a chef and worked in the same kitchen as him. Blake was seeing her every day that she was there. I told him I was going to leave him, but he begged me not to and promised me he would end it. I think he became scared.

Shortly after that he had to go away for a two-week spell training on Salisbury Plain. One day while he was away I had been to the shops and while walking back I heard a voice shout to me, 'Are you called Jeanette?'

I said 'Oh, you're Anna, aren't you?'

I knew straight away that it was Anna. I recognised her from the photograph. I suggested she walk back with me and she did. She told me Blake had told her that it was all over between us and that we'd separated. She told me that he hadn't ended it, that it was still going on, but she promised me that she would end it right away.

When he came back from his training he must have got the message that she had dumped him properly because he started crawling to me. It came out that she had started to see someone else. It was a Staff Sergeant who was even older than Blake. I had heard about this, but Blake didn't know I knew. He came home from work this one particular day and he was so down in the dumps, he was in a foul mood. He had found out that this girl was seeing his Staff Sergeant, in his kitchen. He'd seen her in a yellow convertible car side by side with his Staff Sergeant.

His attitudes changed all the time depending on what was going on in his life. Not long after this affair had ended he said he wanted us to have another baby, so we tried for one and then when I did get pregnant his mood changed again. He told me to get rid of it.

I half-suspected he might have found some other girl, because he would go off for ages down to the phone box on the site, even though we had a phone in the house. He'd also go off to the block where the lads lived, saying he was going to watch the football with them. He would be gone all day and all night and come back in the early hours of the morning. It was things like that that made me suspicious.

He was also probably feeling trapped, because having another baby would tie him down even more and he didn't like the idea of having his freedom taken away. Not that it had ever bothered him much up to then. I refused to get rid of it.

We were then moved again to another house, a bigger house at Bulford because we were soon going to have two children. This house was on the outskirts of the camp in a section of army quarters that was normally reserved for officers and non-commissioned officers. It didn't go down too well us moving in and we were generally ignored by most of the other residents. The kids were also horrible to Hayley because her mum and dad weren't officer ranked.

About this time Blake had to go away on manoeuvres for two weeks and I was getting bigger and bigger, and when he came back he announced that he would soon be going off to serve in Bosnia. When he did go, he didn't leave me any money at all. He took his bank cards with him and I was left to manage on just the family allowance, which was nowhere near enough.

Luckily all our bills were paid for by the army, such as gas and electricity, but I still had to find money for food for Hayley and myself. I would go down to the local mini-store on the camp and I had to watch every penny.

Because Blake was away on tour, he got an allowance from his wages and the rest was stacked up for when he came back. It was done like that because there was no-where for them to spend anything out there. But I had no access to any of his money – wages or anything!

I was really struggling, a single mum and pregnant with no income. I approached the army through the families' officer, but I was told there was nothing they could do. They did help later after I'd been in Salisbury Hospital a couple of times with severe constipation and dehydration through not being able to look after myself. I was put on drips to rehydrate me and to get my sugar levels up.

Because I was in hospital for a couple of weeks, it was decided that Hayley would come up to Leyland and stay with Bradley and Angie. My mum didn't want to look after her and there was nobody else.

Prior to me being admitted to hospital, there were times when Hayley – bless her – would say when I would put her food in front of her (and there wasn't much), 'You have some mummy' and I would say No but she would insist. She would say, 'Let's share, you have some and I'll have some.'

She was only four at that time, and I had to take a little bit off her spoon otherwise she wouldn't have any.

When I came home from hospital, I was visited by the army's health officer. Seeing the way things were, they managed to contact Blake, and he eventually agreed to let me have £50 a week. They couldn't have forced him to give it me; they weren't allowed to do that, but I think they must have shamed him into it. I then managed to get a free train ticket from the army to come home to collect Hayley. One of the wives of another soldier friend of Blake's travelled up with me. When we got home we found out Angie and Bradley had gone out to the Navy Club and had left Blake's two younger brothers looking after Hayley, which was OK because they were older by now and quite capable.

I went round to the Navy Club to see Angie and Bradley and Bradley was very drunk. He loved Navy Rum and drank lots of it, and so did Angie. I started to explain about my pregnancy and they got very irate. An argument started, they were accusing me of playing around and said the baby I was carrying wasn't Blake's. I told them some home truths about what he'd been up to, but they wouldn't have any of it.

They made out that I was playing around – because there were two of us, young girls from an army camp and out on our own, we had to be up to no good!

I later went back to their house to get Hayley and as soon as we got through the door the argument started again and they started slapping me and calling me all sorts. Then Bradley dragged me upstairs to the back bedroom and forced me down. He pinned me down while Angie had a go at knocking hell out of me. I was trying to get up, I was biting them and screaming. I even tried to climb out of the bedroom window at one point, but Bradley had nailed the windows down. They locked me in and left me there.

I must have cried myself to sleep that night, and when I woke up the following morning I was covered in cuts and bruises and I had foot marks all over me, even on my stomach and legs. How I hadn't lost my baby, I don't know. The girl I was with just stayed out of it all and when I came downstairs the morning after, Bradley and Angie acted as if nothing had happened.

I went straight back down south to Bulford, taking Hayley with me. As soon as I got back I contacted the police. They came round and interviewed me and took photographs of the marks on my body. One photograph was a perfect imprint of the sole of Bradley's shoe on the back of my leg. I was definitely pressing charges. As far as I was concerned Bradley was going down for that. Beating up a pregnant woman was a serious offence.

I had to have a scan on the baby because I was having pains and losing blood. The scan showed the bag she was in was hanging out of my womb, and things were quite serious for a while. She is lucky to be here. We're not sure if the problems she has in her life now were caused by what happened that night, but there is a good chance it did contribute to them.

Blake eventually came home on two weeks leave.He was fully aware of what had happened and he was quite supportive at first, saying things like, 'Too right you're going to press charges, just wait till I see them.'

But then one day, he had a phone call from his mum. She was crying and said she had been really ill. She'd had yellow jaundice and gallstones and was so worried about Bradley's case, so much so that it was making her ill and she didn't know if she was going to live or not.

Straight away his attitude changed and he told me I had to drop all the charges. It wasn't open for discussion, he had made his mind up and I had to do as I was told. I was bloody angry about it, but what could I do? He got his way. I went to the police and I dropped the charges. The police tried to talk me out of doing it, but I had no choice, he was such a dominant man. I didn't speak to Bradley and Angie for a long time after that.

Blake hadn't been home from Bosnia long when the baby was due to be born and when the time did come he had managed to get time off work. Because I'd had a section with my first baby, I was given the option of having a section this time and I took that option. On the day I was due to go into Salisbury General Hospital he decided he wasn't going to come with me and he left me to catch the bus to the hospital on my own with my case. It wasn't until it was all over with that he finally showed up. Emma Louise was born on 3rd March 1997. He came back a couple of nights later with one of his mates, Rick, who had been one of our witnesses at our wedding and he said he had decided we were going to call the baby Emma. They had come up with the name because of the Spice Girl Emma Bunton (Baby Spice). I was only in hospital for a couple of days on that occasion.

It was only a few months after giving birth to Emma that I found out I was pregnant again. Blake was due to go to Kenya on a three-month exercise. When I told him he made it quite clear that I would have to get rid of it. I said I didn't want to because I didn't believe in abortion.

'Tough, you're having an abortion and that's that, you get rid of it or I'll get rid of it for you', he said; he made a very big issue of it.

He went off to Kenya, and had a pretty bad experience while he was out there. One of his mates had gone missing and they had to search for him. He was found dead after about three days, and this really upset Blake. He wasn't out there long, but when he got back he started again, saying I had to get rid of it. I was about 11 weeks pregnant at this point. He was so adamant that I wasn't having this baby, he even kicked me in the stomach and jumped on my belly to try to cause me to have a miscarriage. Eventually I had to give in and we went down to the clinic and all the arrangements were made. He made out to the doctors that it was something we both wanted, saying we had discussed it and it was what we had both agreed. It was booked in quite soon because of the stage of the pregnancy. It was a same day procedure. I remember the night before I had it done, I was in the bath and I cried and cried my eyes out.

After the procedure had been done and we left the hospital you could see the difference in him. It was as if all his 'pretend cares' had vanished. He was striding out and I was in quite a bit of pain. I was pretty tender and all he could do was curse and swear at me, telling me to, 'Fucking hurry up, get a fucking move on', as he raced towards the bus stop. When I got home, I felt that something wasn't right. I was still having bad pains. I was in agony. This went on for a few days, but all he could say was, I was a hypochondriac.

I was in so much pain, so I waited until he'd gone to work and I rang and made an appointment to see the doctor and he sent me to hospital. He got one of the drivers to take me. Little did they know that I'd got the bus home from hospital earlier. When I got to hospital they did a scan and found that there was still some of the baby in there. I had to go through it all again and have the same procedure.

Blake had been told that I had been taken to hospital and he came over; he was quite all right about it. It meant he could have time off work. It didn't mean anything to him that I was having all this trouble, but once at the hospital he made it clear that he was going to take this further as it was negligence on the hospital's part. He was really playing up the concerned husband routine. The truth was, he couldn't care less!

I was lucky that he had gone to work that day because if he hadn't, there would have been no way he would have let me see a doctor or come to hospital. He would have made me put up with the pain and the truth is it could have killed me. I became so depressed after all this, that I was taking Prozac.

I just didn't want to live, and he didn't give a shit. There were days when I was no better than a zombie. I would go to bed and just lie there and stare into space and everything sounded so loud.

When I eventually got myself feeling better, I realised from that point just how much I absolutely hated him and I wished him dead. He was even being an evil swine with Emma. He was OK with Hayley, she could do no wrong, she was his little princess and could have anything she wanted, but it was as if Emma didn't belong.

I used to lie in bed and imagine killing him. Then one night when he was drunk and fast asleep I put my hand over his mouth and nose, but then he let out a loud snort. I thought, Oh shit! I pulled my hand away and quickly turned over, it scared me to death, but lucky for me he didn't wake up.

He had treated me so badly during our time together. There had been times when he would come home drunk, and would force me out of bed and onto the floor to sleep. I did it just to keep the peace, but then that might not be enough; when he could see that I wasn't arguing he would drag me into the bathroom and make me sleep in there and sometimes even in the bath itself. I have spent the night in the tiny little toilet before now, sat there shivering all night because I knew if I said anything he would hit me.

I felt so much hatred for him and it was all because he had made me have that abortion. I had been to the families' officer a few times whenever there was trouble or a fight between us, and they would then call him in, but all they did was give him a bollocking and belittle him. That was all very well, but he would then take it out on me. I was in a no-win situation. I also began to get the feeling that they thought I was the cause of the problem or that I was making it up. Blake was feeling like the families' officer had it in for him too and he put in for what is known as 'Preference Posting'. It was a request to be posted away.

8

Germany

When Emma was about ten months old, we were informed that his request for a pref posting had been accepted and he was being posted to Germany, and the children and myself were going too. In my foolish way I half-hoped things might be better over there with a fresh start and all that. We travelled over as a family, flying from Stansted Airport in an army Tristar. The plane was strange; you had to sit facing the back. It was my first ever experience of flying.

A couple of days before we were due to go all our furniture was packed into army wagons and went ahead of us. We were just left with the very basic essentials to get us through. We even had to sleep on just a mattress; we didn't have any other furniture apart from a settee and a cooker, and they belonged to the army.

On the Friday as our stuff was being packed to go to Germany, Angie and Bradley came down to take Hayley and Emma back north for the weekend. I still hated Bradley for what he had done to me the year before, but I put up with the situation.

On the night before we were due to go Blake had been out drinking as usual and had come back expecting me to be the loving little wife; he was all over me trying to have his way, but there was no way I was going to go along with it. I was determined and told him so. I wasn't in any fit state for that and I hated him so much for making me have the termination that I had decided that I wasn't going to be used any more.

As usual he started on me; he hit me, but he made sure he stayed away from my face so I wouldn't have any visible bruises, but he slapped both his hands on the side of my head. It was so loud and I thought my head was going to burst. The following morning I was well out of it and my head was banging. The flight was awful and when we had got to Germany I ended up at the doctors within a couple of days.

The doctor examined me and told me I had burst both my eardrums. He asked if I knew how I could have done that. I said the flight over had been bad with a lot of turbulence, but he dismissed that straight away. He asked if I'd had any ear infections and I told him I hadn't. It was all because Blake had bashed my ears the night before we left, but I didn't tell him that was the reason.

When we arrived in Germany we had flown to Hanover and we were met by an army driver who took us to where we were staying. He introduced us to the families' officer first and then took us to our accommodation which was in a large block of flats.

The address was 1-3 Kant-Strasse. We were in Flat 1 on the third floor. The block was six floors high but at one point they had decided to empty the whole block and demolish it. But they had only cleared the top two floors and left it at that.

Kant-Strasse was in a normal rural area about a mile from the army camp, but our block was all soldiers. Across the way there were civilians including some Turks and some Croatians. Some of those people were so poor, we used to see them rummaging around in the bins outside the apartment block on the site. They would be looking for stuff they could sell for scrap.

On the day we arrived, we were being shown up to our apartment on the third floor, and the first person we met was Chris, who was just putting some bottles out. He smiled and said hello and I remember thinking what a lovely smile he had and what a happy person he seemed. And I thought, Wow, he's sweet, and then I checked myself for thinking such things when I was married.

We went to our flat and had a look around; it was already carpeted and there was a cooker installed. Our furniture was due to arrive the following day so we just had to make do with what we had for that first night. In no time at all, we were soon mixing with the others from the block and especially Chris and his wife. Chris had asked his wife to come up and introduce herself to us. She did and brought us tea and coffee which I thought was really nice. There was another couple in Flat 1-1 on the first floor next to Chris. Again, he was a soldier and his wife was a German girl; they were great fun.

I had suspected before we left England that Blake had started messing around with another girl and my suspicions grew when we had moved to Germany. We were getting on so well with our new neighbours and we would get together for a drink in one another's flats a few evenings a week and we also used to have barbecues outside on the back field. All the men would be at work and I was sometimes literally dragged down the stairs to join in.

'C'mon, come down and have something to eat with us; have a drink', they'd say. And in one way I felt I had to otherwise it would have looked as though I didn't want to mix and make friends, but I did, I really did. I was a long way from home and living with a violent man so I needed friends.

I wanted to join in, but I knew it was against all that Blake believed in. In his eyes I should be at home waiting for him with his meal on the table when he got home from work, but in one way his meal was ready for him because we had done a barbecue. All the kids would be playing, and they would get the paddling pools out and everyone would be having a good time. We all got on like a house on fire but I could see from the look in Blake's eyes that he wasn't happy about things.

Things were getting much worse over in Germany. Blake's moods were worse and I was in constant fear of him. Most wives would have been looking forward to their husbands coming in from work in the evening, but I was terrified. I was still in my routine of checking everything to make sure it was all in place before he walked in. I would check and double-check, then check again. I knew if he could find the slightest thing to pick an argument, he would.

I also used to make sure Emma was safely tucked away in bed before he came home, because he would pick on her for the smallest of things and I was so fearful that one day he might hurt her. It was of course completely different with Hayley; she could do no wrong in his eyes.

There were nights when Blake would tell me to go down to Chris's flat for a drink with Chris and his wife. I didn't always want to go, but Blake could be quite insistent when he wanted to be and I began to wonder if he was trying to get me out of the flat so he could ring this girl back in England. I found out later that I was right, he was ringing her.

During our time in Germany, I think it was a couple of months after we'd moved there, I was having some problems down below and I had to have some tests done, and the doctors found I had cervical problems. The tests showed that if I didn't have treatment, it could develop into cancer. I was sent to have a small biopsy and then for a massive cone-biopsy.

The tests showed that I needed to have some treatment in my belly and this was the same treatment that they use to treat breast cancer; it's called Zoladex. What this does is make you go through a kind of menopause. It stops everything from working. So I had to go into hospital and have this done.

At the time, Blake had been sent away on some exercises and he'd been away for a couple of weeks, and when he got back he was just his usual self in that he didn't care what I'd been through or how I was feeling. He hadn't been in the flat for more than a few minutes, he'd said hello to Hayley – hardly bothered with Emma or me and then taken himself off to the pub.

When he got back later that night he was his usual bolshie self and started wanting to have his way with me. I told he couldn't because I was bleeding after my treatment, but it made no difference to him, he still wanted it. He tried and then when he realised he couldn't because there was so much blood he raped me from my back passage and that was really bad. It made me hate him even more.

The violence had always been bad, but it seemed to get worse as time wore on. There was another incident, not long after he'd raped me where we had all gone out one night to a bar for a drink and there was karaoke on. I'd always liked singing and I was pretty good, so the rest of them all started egging me on to have a go, so I did; I got up and sang, but all the time I could see the look on Blake's face – he was giving me looks that said 'Get down here now' (like you would tell a dog) so I did as I was told, and when I sat down I could feel him kicking my chair the whole time. I had won a bottle of champagne for best singer; I was really chuffed, but that seemed to make him even worse, and he got up and said, 'Come on, we're going'. I had to do as I was told so I said goodnight to the others and we left.

Once out in the street he went mad at me. He smashed the bottle of champagne that I'd won and then he laid in to me, hitting me and he dragged me down the street by my hair. He bashed my head on the kerb and I was dazed and bleeding pretty badly; my teeth were broken. Another soldier shouted at him and asked him what he was doing. He shouted back at him saying, 'What the hell has it got to do with you?'

A fight broke out between them and as all this was going on I crawled across the road and a German couple took me into their house and called the army police. By the time they arrived the fight was over and Blake had gone. They took me back home and found Blake in bed. They got him out of there and locked him up.

The following day we had to go and see the families' officer and Chris and the others had also been called in separately because they had all been out with us as couples. Until then none of the others had any idea about Blake's violence towards me. It seemed to upset Chris, because he'd had no idea and if he had known, he would have looked out for me. He was quite a big lad and worked as an engineer/mechanic. He worked on tanks.

I decided to tell the families' officer about how Blake had raped me a couple of nights before. He was furious with Blake and suggested we go away and that he should consider his actions. He told him he would be going to Kosovo soon and that this wasn't an excuse to change that and it wouldn't change that, he would still be going; I was glad that he was. The officer said we should try to resolve matters between us before he went away. The result of that talk was that I got another good hiding that night. It was my birthday that night, 28th July; I was twenty-one. He had picked up a table and thrown it at my leg. It hit me and made a right mess of my leg; right on the shinbone. After Blake had beaten me up and locked me in the flat I couldn't get out and he had taken the phone and hidden it. I eventually did find it and I called the guard room.

I didn't know, but Chris was the NCO in the guard room that night and he came round with the van and got me out. They then went off searching the streets looking for Blake. Chris arrested him that night and once the guards had him in the cells they gave him a good hiding. It wasn't Chris, but some of the other guards who had heard about the violence I'd had to put up with.

Once things had calmed down the regular get-togethers in each other's flats carried on, but there were some nights when Blake would tell me to go down to have a drink with Chris and his wife; he would practically order me to. It was his doing this that made me think he was up to something. We had a landline in our flat and whenever the bill came he paid it and he made sure I didn't get to see it.

I would go downstairs and we always had a good laugh. I think Chris went out of his way to cheer me up, knowing what life was like for me. One particular night when we'd been having a right giggle and I was making my way back upstairs Blake was standing waiting on the stairs.

'You were having a good old time down there, weren't you?'

But you don't go out to be morbid, do you? After all, it was his idea for me to go down to their flat. I thought afterwards that he did it just to get me out of the flat so he could ring this girl back in England. I also began to suspect he'd had an argument with her and maybe he was taking it out on me.

The final straw happened one night. I had come back to our flat from spending an hour downstairs. Blake was there on the stairwell and in a really foul mood. I found out later that she had dumped him over the phone and he took it out on me. He was accusing me of having an affair, which was ridiculous. I wouldn't have done anything like that – I wouldn't have dared to.

I had gone into the kitchen to make a cup of tea and I asked Blake if he wanted one. He said he didn't, but I knew what he was like and if I didn't make him one he would tell me to make him one afterwards so I made him one anyway. He was standing behind me at the time and he was filling his lighter. I could smell this fuel really strongly; I turned round and he was spraying this tin of lighter fuel all over me.

It was all over my woolly cardigan, in my hair and all over me. He carried on spraying it at me, it was going in my eyes and my mouth and I couldn't see or breathe properly for all this petrol; I was covered in it. I was screaming and jumping around making a lot of noise. I was hoping that someone would hear me and come and help me, and all the time he was shouting at me that he was going to kill me.

He began to flick his lighter slowly and in a very menacing way and he kept repeating, 'I'm going to do it … I am … I'm going to kill you.' Over and over he kept repeating it and I was pleading and begging for my life. I had dropped down to my knees and all these millions of thoughts went through my mind so quickly, and all I could see were red and white flashes before my eyes – big red ones, then big white ones over and over again.

I put my hands together and I was praying out loud to God to save me, not to let him kill me. I was by now dripping in petrol. One of the strangest things was that I felt like I was having an out of body experience. It was as if I was in the room looking down on myself knelt there praying. I have never experienced anything like that in my life, it was so weird.

Suddenly he stopped flicking his lighter, it was as if he was in shock at seeing me so terrified; he just stopped and walked away into the other room. I seemed to stay there for ages, too scared to move. Then I heard him crying like a baby. I eventually got up and went in to where he was. He was sobbing and asking me to forgive him. He had done some pretty mad things over the years, but nothing as mad as that. That was close to murder.

I did feel bad for him even though he'd just done that

to me. I had never seen him cry like that before. I sat there at the side of him and he was cuddling me and crying. After a while I got up and went to get changed. It was still in my mind that he could have a change of mind and set fire to me; I was still soaked in petrol and it would only take a spark.

All throughout that night he was so apologetic, he just kept saying how sorry he was, all night. But I knew then that I had to get away from him somehow and I lay there with my eyes open all night imagining ways of how I would leave him. I could visualise myself walking out of the bedroom towards the door and then suddenly his hands would be on me. It was so bad that I felt the only way I would ever escape would be if I killed him. He had broken me, I was a wreck. It had become that bad. I was mentally and physically drained.

It was only a matter of days after that that he was posted to Kosovo, and I knew then that I would have to think seriously about leaving him before he came back. He was due to be out there for three months. Just before he went, we were due to go before the families' officer again. We had to attend this because there had been an appointment made for us and if we hadn't gone we would have been in trouble. Especially Blake! He begged me not to say anything about the petrol incident, but I did; I wanted it all out in the open. The officer was completely unaware of this, and his face dropped. He told Blake that when he did come back from Kosovo he would have to have some counselling. I felt like it was me who needed the counselling.

I didn't know at the time, but things hadn't been going too well with Chris and his wife at the same time. The only difference was, Chris wasn't the violent type. Things must have got to the point where Chris couldn't take any more and he moved out. I was still friends with them both and I still carried on being friends with his wife and would go down there for a natter and a coffee.

One day she told me she had a woman coming over who was a psychic medium, her name was Erica. I don't think she was German, but she did have some kind of foreign accent. She was going to give her a reading, and I asked if she would do the same for me. The woman came and I asked her if she would do a reading for me too, but she said, 'No, I will do yours tomorrow and I want you to come to a different place.' I assumed she must have been busy, so I didn't give it any thought. I made arrangements to see her the following day and I got a taxi to an address she had given me. It was a house where she stayed when she was visiting this area. She led me into a bedroom and we sat down.

She began to tell me of all the incidents that had happened to me. She knew all about Blake and the violence. She knew about me having the abortion and how much it had made me hate Blake. She even knew about the petrol incident just a few weeks before. I had told no one about any of these events – how could she possibly have known?

She warned me that I must leave Blake before a certain date at the end of August that year or I would be dead. I believed her because she had told me so much about myself that nobody could possibly have known. The end of August coincided with Blake's leave. He was due to come home for a short break part-way through his tour of duty in Kosovo. She went on to say that I would find happiness, she said I would meet a nice man who was also in the army and that he was in some way attached to tanks. She said we would make our home in England.

At the time I didn't connect the fact that Chris worked on tanks and even though he and his wife had split up there had not been anything between Chris and me. I did on one occasion feel very sorry for him. I was in his flat having a coffee with his wife when he came round to see his kids.

She wouldn't let him see them and she grabbed hold of him, pushed him against the wall and kneed him right between the legs, then as he was going down the hallway she picked up a huge plant pot that was full of soil and plants and threw it at him; it just missed his head. She was quite a big girl with a lot of red hair and she obviously had a very nasty streak.

I hated seeing people fight, I think it was because of all the stuff that had happened between Blake and me – it made me nervous and it still does! I had no idea that things were as bad as this between Chris and his wife – just like he didn't know what was going on with Blake and me.

With Blake now out of the way, I had made up my mind what I wanted to do. I went round to see the families' officer again and this time I told him that I wanted to leave Blake and that I wouldn't be coming back again. He asked me if I was sure it was what I wanted and I assured him it was.

I asked if the army could give me any assistance to get me and my two girls back to England and he said that wouldn't be a problem; I also asked him about my furniture. He said he could have that sent over to me once I was settled.

I came away from the families' officer feeling that at last I was going to be rid of the monster. He had been controlling me since I was thirteen and I'd had to put up with some pretty horrific situations, such as him trying to drown me in the bath, locking me in the bathroom all night and having to sleep in a small box-room toilet. He would come home late from the pub and bring a gang of his mates back. He would get me up out of bed to make them something to eat. He was nothing more or less than an animal. He had made me so ill. At one point I was becoming anorexic, it was Chris's wife who made me go to the doctor and get myself sorted out. It was all down to the stress that I was under.

Then when he made me have an abortion I finally re-alised how much I hated him, but the final straw was the incident with the petrol. I knew then, that if I didn't get away from him, he would kill me.

I went back home to the flat that afternoon and I saw all my neighbours and explained that I was leaving. I also saw Chris and told him I was leaving, and he asked me if he could look me up when I got settled. I told him I would like that. He offered to bring some of my stuff back over to England the next time he was coming over. I asked him if he would be able to drop my TV off and he said he would.

9

Coming home

Everything moved very fast. Our flights back home were arranged for the following day. I packed our suitcases and rang my mum to tell her everything that had happened. She was shocked because I'd told her hardly anything of what had gone on with Blake; she knew he had been violent with me, but she didn't know about the abortion or the petrol, and she really only knew about a few of the fights that had gone on.

She arranged for the husband of a friend of hers to drive down to Stansted to collect us. The poor guy didn't know where he was going and it was just the same coming back – neither of us knew which way to go. It was the blind leading the blind.

When we touched down in the UK it felt so good to be back and away from Blake. I knew he would be due some leave from Kosovo at some point, and I knew darned well he would come looking for me. When we got back home the girls and I stayed at my mum's, and I wasn't wrong, he did turn up during his period of leave.

When he knocked at the door, I answered it and refused to let him in. Although he had been so violent in the past, I felt quite safe because I knew my family were there and I knew he wouldn't try anything. He stood on the doorstep pleading with me to go back to him. He was crying and making all sorts of promises, but as far as I was concerned there was nothing left between us. I was just so glad that it was all finally over. I shut the door and felt a huge sense of relief.

Also, just before Blake had come back. Chris had been over to see me; we had kept in touch, writing and phoning each other ever since I had left Germany. He was due to have four weeks' summer leave and was planning to go to see his mother in Northern Ireland, but said he would like to come and see me before he went over there.

He had driven over, bringing his wife over to her mother's in Reading. She was at the time considering moving back to the UK too. His marriage was completely broken down by now.He drove up to Leyland and brought me my television. We met up and he took me to Blackpool for a few days. My mum had agreed to look after Hayley and Emma for the weekend. They had gone down to Skegness for a short holiday and Chris and I ran the kids down there to meet my mum and then we went straight to Blackpool. At that point Chris had not met my mum. We were just friends at this stage. We knew we liked one another and we were both single, but had agreed to take it easy and see how things went.

Chris had left his wife long before I left Blake, but we didn't want to rush into anything at that point. Before Chris went over to his mum's in Belfast, he had offered to take me back to Germany to collect some more of my belongings that Blake was holding on to. We knew Blake was still in Bosnia, so I agreed and took the ferry over to Ireland to meet Chris's mum and dad. His mum was pretty wary about me at that stage and gave Chris a stiff talking to.

'I hope you're not up to anything with this young lass? You're still married and you both have children to consider.' She really had a go at him.

I stayed for a couple of days and then we came back to England to pick up Chris's car and we drove to Germany.

It was a hell of a journey going over there and back in one weekend, and I was scared even though I knew Blake wasn't there. I still felt very fearful entering the flat again and I couldn't wait to get out of there.

Chris was due to go to Canada for a six-week tour of duty when he rejoined his unit. During the time I'd been home I had got onto the housing register for a place of my own. The army had offered me a place in Manchester, but I turned it down; it felt too far away and I still didn't feel safe knowing Blake was out there somewhere. They also offered me a place in Preston, but I turned that down too.

Eventually the council found me a place in Leyland on Robin Hey, which was in the Moss Side area – not that far away from my mum's, so that wasn't so bad. I found it to be quite an isolated, un-neighbourly area, where nobody bothered with anyone, but I intended to keep myself to myself anyway.

I took the house and contacted the army to ask where my furniture was; they said they would sort it, but nothing happened; I did get some help through the Royal British Legion. They managed to get me a cooker and a washer. I had an old brown settee that was literally falling to pieces, and a really thin carpet.

During those first few months at Robin Hey I still spent a lot of time round at my mum's. I was still very nervous of being on my own. I would keep the curtains closed and constantly check that the doors were locked. I was still very obsessive about checking things all the time. I would go to bed and run upstairs and quickly turn the lights out and then put them on again and go back down to check the doors again, that's how bad I was. I even had the police domestic violence officer come round and install panic alarms because I was so afraid of what might happen if Blake turned up, but I was still scared, even with all that.

I'd been in Robin Hey for a while and had been think-ing that Chris must have forgotten about me. I hadn't heard anything from him for a good few weeks and certainly nothing since he'd been in Canada. I was sure he must have lost interest and began to think that was that. Then one day out of the blue, I was busy doing some decorating when my mum rang me to say she'd had a call from Chris. She had given him my number and he was going to ring me, so I should be receiving a call from him anytime.

That really threw me and yet I was so excited at the thought that he still wanted to see me – he was still interested. His date for coming back from Canada was somewhere around the end of October 1999. He had said he wanted to come straight to me. Then the thought hit me about the state of my house. I was so embarrassed; I hardly had anything in the house apart from that old settee and a few other bits. What would Chris think when he saw how I was living?

Suddenly one day I got a phone call to say that my furniture was due to arrive before the end of the week; I was so relieved. On the Friday of that week a huge army wagon pulled up at my door. When they opened it up all I'd got was a couple of boxes with the children's clothes and toys, a bunk bed that Blake had purposely smashed in half and broken all the slats, and a chest of drawers with the bottoms punched through; and I just sat there on the stairs and cried.

I rang the families' officer in Germany and asked where my three-piece suite was and my table and chairs and other stuff. He said he didn't know, but he would make some enquiries and get back to me. He rang me back later and told me that Blake had sold it all and there was nothing he could do about that. He said that it was Blake's to sell if he chose to, and he could only send me what he had been given. I was devastated.

Chris was the most understanding and laid back bloke I'd ever met. I was so worried about what he would think, but he just told me it was me he'd come to see and he didn't care about material things like that. By now, Chris's mum had come round to the idea that we were keen on one another and Chris had told her about my furniture situation. She sent me a beautiful cabinet with her best wishes, hoping it would cheer me up, and it did. Chris was fantastic with me and the girls; he very soon put me at ease. It was around Bonfire Night, 5th November. We had made plans to go to the park to see the bonfire and watch the fireworks display.

It was a horrible wet night. Chris was holding Emma on one arm and had his other arm around me. He suddenly kissed me on my head. Emma saw this and gave him a look as if to say, 'Why are you kissing my mummy like that?' We both laughed.

My mum was with us and she could see that we were becoming very fond of each other. She offered to have the kids for the night and Chris came back with me to my house at Robin Hey and that was the first time we spent the night together properly as a couple.

Chris went back to Germany after that weekend, but by now we were so much in love that he would come over to England every weekend. We also had a huge shock because I found out I had become pregnant literally as soon as we had got together, probably on that very first night. I was a bit annoyed at first, but it was to be and we accepted it.

Chris's wife was again making trouble for him. She had decided she wanted to move back to Germany. She had contacted the army who said it was still down to Chris to sort out, even though he felt it was nothing to do with him. So the army allowed her to go back to Germany for three months during which time Chris had to give her £200 a week for her accommodation and her bills, and he still had to look after himself.

Chris couldn't cope; I was helping him as much as I could so we were both struggling. In the end he told the army he wanted a move back over here to Warminster. The army agreed, but he still had to pay for his wife's accommodation, and by this point, her three months were up and yet she still needed somewhere to live. She decided that she wanted to move back to the UK. But she wanted to go to Scotland.

The army moved her back and found her a place in Scotland. It was on the Airforce base at Kinloss, but Chris still had to pay for her accommodation and her bills. That just left Chris about £50 a month after he'd paid for her and paid for his own keep. I sent him some money down once a fortnight to help with his petrol so he could come up to Leyland to see me. All the time this was going on Chris wasn't allowed to see his kids. He had two children, a boy and a girl. His wife was so vindictive that she wouldn't let him anywhere near them. She had said to him, 'You're not seeing the kids as long as you're with her', meaning me! That, along with having to pay for her keep was beginning to break Chris, but even with all this our relationship was strong. I knew it wasn't fair, the kids needed to see their father and he them, and in a way I felt I was to blame, but Chris never once suggested that; totally the opposite.

Even though I was now in a happy relationship with Chris and I knew he would never harm me, I was still fearful of Blake coming round, and I only really felt comfortable when Chris was with me.

I was still going through my routine of checking and double-checking all the doors and windows every night and when I'd had a cigarette, I was constantly checking that it had been put out properly, stubbing it and stubbing it and then putting it in water. All that had stemmed from the incident with the petrol in Germany. My fear of fire is still with me today, but not quite as bad as it was.

When Chris was home my obsession with checking the doors was still there, but I didn't run up the stairs after putting the light out any more. Chris would walk up behind me and keep me calm. It took me a long time to get over the violence I'd had to put up with during all those years with Blake.

Having had just about as much as he could take, Chris finally got enough money together to buy himself out of the army. He couldn't take any more and apart from that, he wanted to be with me in Leyland. During the final few weeks of his service while he was waiting for his discharge to come through, the families' officer had made his life hell.

He had learned that legally, he didn't have to pay for his wife's keep for any longer than 92 days, but unknown to him, Chris's Captain in the army had signed a document in Chris's name allowing his wife to have all the privileges for a further 92 days.

When he kicked up a fuss about this and questioned it, he was told by the Captain that if he didn't stop questioning his actions he would be put under close arrest. Chris's Warrant Officer at the time had a talk to him and said, 'This army is no good for you Chris, I am getting out myself as soon as I can', and that made Chris's mind up for him.

He left the army in March 2000, came home and moved in with me at Robin Hey. For a while it was great, it was a bit like a holiday, but then he needed a job. He managed to get a part-time job at a place called First Class Response, a card-packing company. He didn't like it, but he got on with it. I was also working there part-time doing the same job.

Then he got an interview for Leyland Trucks, he had to go through some tests and he passed them and started work there. He loved it but that wasn't to last for long before he was laid off. Leyland Trucks had a reputation for taking people on and laying them off just as fast.

I was of course by now very heavily pregnant, and Chris was slowly beginning to realise just how insecure life was outside the army. When you're in the services your job is safe and everything is covered for you, all your bills, your rent, everything! But it's completely different in Civvie Street; it's a whole new ball game. Chris had been in the army since he was eighteen and hadn't known any other way of life. I could see the pressure building on him.

Things did ease for him when our daughter Carrie was born. I had been offered the option of having another section and decided to take it. I had been suffering with a condition called Synthis Pubis which is a pelvic condition in pregnant women. It is quite common, but I was in a lot of pain with it. I was huge and had to have a special tubigrip bandage to help hold up my bump off my pelvis; I also needed crutches to walk.

The doctors had taken the decision to plan the delivery for 37 weeks, so when the time arrived, I was prepared and Chris was looking forward to it happening, but at the same time he was a bit worried about his employment situation and having another mouth to feed, but all those worries soon disappeared when Carrie arrived.

All was arranged and I went into Sharoe Green Hospital at 9 a.m. on 20th July 2000. I got changed and was waiting to go to theatre. The nurse came in and told me there was a delay because of an emergency. 'Great', I thought, I could sneak off for a crafty cig. I had smoked all the way through my pregnancy. I had tried to stop, but couldn't.

I had gone down to the smoking area and hadn't been there above a minute or two when a nurse came running in after me, 'Come on, they're waiting for you', so off back to the ward I went. The consultant was a man, it was the first time I'd had a male consultant. I was given an epidural and was awake all though the procedure. All went well and Carrie was born safely and she was healthy. The doctor held her up for me to see and, I said, 'Oh my God she's so tiny.'

But I hadn't taken into consideration that it was a great big gripper holding on to her with huge hands. She did develop a little bit of jaundice, but that cleared up quickly.

I only stayed in hospital for about three days and then we took her back home to Robin Hey.

We still didn't have much for her, but she did have lots of love. My mum had bought us a lovely new pram out of her catalogue. It was a really stylish one and I was over the moon with it.

I decided to breastfeed Carrie, but had to give up. I was in so much pain trying that I couldn't do it. There was one day I took my bra off to rest my boobs and they were enormous. The midwife came round one day and took one look at them and said, 'Oh my God, love, get some strings put on them.' I asked why. She told me that having my bra off made them fill even more. They were like melons! I was in agony. She suggested I have a bath and massage them down.

I ran myself a nice bath and gently eased myself in. I hadn't been in long when Chris walked in, took one look at me and came out with some ridiculous remark that had me laughing so much it hurt. I was in agony. My boobs were sore and my stitches were pulling, but I couldn't help myself, laughing at what he had called my boobs. I gave up trying to breastfeed after that.

Chris was amazing as a dad; I had never experienced a man being as loving as he was with Carrie. I even got a little jealous because of the way he was with her; he was obsessive, but in a nice way. When I was breastfeeding he would get up in the middle of the night and sit with me wanting to help – I think he would have breastfed her himself if he could.

The job situation was still pretty dire at this point. Chris was doing his best; I was limited to what I could do, because I now had three children to look after. We struggled on as best we could, but by now we were considering other options. Chris suggested he might have more chance of a better job over in Northern Ireland, which is where he is from.

We thought about it for some months. Chris had left Northern Ireland when he was just eighteen to join the army. Although we wouldn't have anywhere to stay if we went, we felt we should give it a go. Chris's mum had said we could stay with her for a while until we could find somewhere of our own.

We decided we would get Christmas out of the way and then make the move.

10

Northern Ireland

When we did decide to go we had very little money and the future was probably going to be just as uncertain over there as it was here, but Chris was becoming very restless and needed the fresh start. But eighteen years away from home was bad enough, let alone having gone away to join the British Army.

Going back for Chris was tough. He had visited for short periods during the time he'd been in the army, and he felt comfortable in his mum's house, but he didn't know how people would react towards him once we had our own place; but it was his home and it would always be home to him. His mum and dad were divorced; his mum lived in Glengormley, his dad in Dundonald.

We moved over in January 2001. We hired a van, packed our furniture and stuff, and off we went. We went to stay with Chris's mum until we could get our own place. I was made to feel very welcome by Chris's family, but we knew that staying there was only temporary and we had put our names down on the registry for a house.

In April 2001 we were offered a house on the Monkstown estate. It had a bit of a reputation for being rough, but you don't know until you actually get there. So we moved in, and quite gullibly Chris and me would talk to anyone and we tried to make friends with the neighbours. It was quite scary with Chris being an ex-soldier and finding out that you have members of a paramilitary organisation as your neighbours.

We had become friendly with people not knowing at the time who, or what they were. When we did find out it made Chris more fearful for my safety, because by now he had got a job and was out all day at work knowing that I was alone at home near to these people. He had a job working as a mechanic at a car garage that repaired Land Rovers – not the sort he had worked on in the army, but the more modern civilian type.

Although the estate was very different to what we'd been used to, in some ways it felt quite safe and secure. There apparently weren't any burglaries or drugpushers, it was all very controlled with punishment being handed out by those in charge. So in some ways we felt safe but we were constantly worried about people knowing about Chris's background with the British army.

At the same time, I had a phone call from Blake, my ex-husband. He had found out that I'd moved away and where I was living. He had got our number and phoned to say he was coming over and that he was going to take Hayley away.

Luckily, Chris's dad had contacts with the police and he knew someone who was in charge of the Port Police. We gave them a photograph of Blake and they put our minds at rest. They assured us that they were used to looking out for terrorists and the like and anybody who they didn't want in, wouldn't get in.

No sooner had that crisis been put to bed than I found myself in another one. One of the people we had got to know who was only a youngish sort of guy would come into our house after Chris had gone to work. His little girl went to the same school as Hayley and he would call and say he would walk up with me.

I never felt comfortable with him. He was one of the local paramilitaries that I had heard of and I knew from what people had said that he was quite highly regarded in the organisation. He became quite intimidating and I didn't know what to do. I told Chris that I wasn't happy him being around, but at the same time, I didn't want to get on the wrong side of him.

But things started to get worse. After a while he started to make suggestions and I felt like he was coming on to me. I told Chris that I didn't like him and that it all seemed a bit odd. I said that I had a feeling he was going to try it on with me, he would talk to me in a sexual way, being very suggestive. Chris's first reaction was that he wanted to go round and thump him, but I couldn't let him do that. I knew if he did, he could end up with a bullet in him.

We had heard gunshots in the area on a few occasions, but we'd been warned never to go outside to see what was going on. It was their punishment routine; it was the way they handled things over there. We had been told anyone who interferes could also end up getting hurt. Both Chris and myself found this very hard. I wasn't the sort of person to ignore someone who was screaming in pain and neither was Chris. It was especially hard for him being an ex-soldier. And it went through my mind that if this guy had taken such a shine to me, what would he do to Chris if he was really determined to have me?

The situation was scary and it got to the point where Chris didn't want to go to work. He didn't want to leave me in the mornings, but he didn't have a choice; we needed the money. The whole way of living was a worry.

We knew we had to do something and it quickly became apparent that the only option was to move back to England. While it was good for Chris to be back near his parents, neither of us were comfortable with where we were living. We started to look online at houses and estate agents around the Leyland area. We decided we wanted to buy a place of our own, somewhere where we could really be settled. We were fed up of moving around from place to place and we certainly didn't want to end up back at Robin Hey again,

We had seen a house in the area I'd been brought up in that looked just right for us, and we made some enquiries about it, but we were told it had gone, so we had to keep looking. In the meantime we decided to move back over to England and stay with my mum for a while, and go with the flow from there. We had no intention of staying there for long. We wanted our own place, and anyway, mum hadn't enough room for all us.

We moved back in October 2001. We had only been back a couple of days when Chris got a call from his dad to say that his beloved Nan had died. We knew she hadn't been well, but she died suddenly and it was a real shock.

I remember meeting her and from day one she told me she liked me. She said I was good for her grandson, much better than his last wife because all she ever wanted was his money. She was a lovely old lady who had a way with words. Very straight; she spoke her mind and didn't care if it upset those in the firing line.

It was hard for Chris losing his Nan so suddenly like that. We didn't have much money and having spent a lot on coming back over here, it meant he couldn't go back over for the funeral.

In the first week we arrived back Chris managed to get a job working for a company called Benson's on a building site as a ground worker. It was heavy and demanding work, but it meant we had money coming in. At the same time we were still looking on the internet for a house and were surprised to see that the house that we had been interested in when we were still in Ireland was back on the market.

We made enquiries and found out that the people who were buying it had a problem raising the deposit. The house was up for sale for £39,000 and we needed a deposit of £4,000. Chris very reluctantly asked his dad for a loan, which he agreed to with no quibbles. But we then found ourselves in a bidding war with someone else. We thought 'Oh no, not again!' Luckily for us, they couldn't raise the deposit and we got the house.

We signed up for it at the beginning of November 2001. As it stood, it needed a hell of a lot of work doing to it. Poor Chris was working very long hours on the building site and then coming home and starting all over again. We wanted to get it liveable in time for Christmas and we did, but it still needed loads doing to it. I did my bit in between looking after the kids and everything else.

Although it was a great feeling to own our own house, there was also this feeling that we had all this debt around our necks. As well as having to buy the materials we needed to do the work on the house, Chris's main concern was to pay his dad back as soon as he could. Not that Chris's dad had put any pressure on us for the money, it was just the way Chris wanted to do it.

As well as all that Chris still had debts and family commitments from his first marriage to contend with as well as our normal day to day bills. I didn't help the situation because I had never been in this position before. All I could see was this huge debt around our necks. I didn't realise that what we were paying for our mortgage was probably less than we would have been paying in rent on a property. But I was struggling to cope, and it was around this time that I started to depend on over the counter codeine drugs to help me keep going. This was to be the start of a ten-year addiction.

I worried about all this a lot, thinking I would have all this debt around my neck for the rest of my life and I suppose foolishly and naively I contributed to causing Chris even more stress. We were both stretched mentally and physically at that point, but at first I didn't realise just how badly all this was getting to Chris. It was only gradually that I began to notice a change in him.

11

2002 to 2004:
a really bad time for us

2002 should have been a good year for us – a new house and a new beginning, but it was far from that. There seemed to be a huge cloud over our lives at this point and although neither of us realised it at the time it was a culmination of different events that had happened in our lives. You would think that moving into a new house would have brought happiness, but it hadn't – at least not right away.

In Chris's case it was largely due to having to work extra hard to keep us and pay the bills. It was also down to my being ill, but mainly because of the way his life had been turned upside down. He had always had the security of the army behind him before.

When a man is in the army for as long as Chris was, their life is very routine. Everything they do every day is pre-planned for them, from getting up at a set time, having a shave every day, and even the set times they have a meal. They are treated like children in a way and they know that if there are any problems there is a team behind them to help sort it out.

His problems had begun well before he got together with me. He had been involved in an accident in Germany when a Land Rover he was travelling in overturned in a ditch. Chris was injured in the crash; he had a dislocated shoulder, head injuries and concussion. There had been four of them in the vehicle at the time. They were being transported to a firing range. The driver of the Land Rover was drunk at the time and the officer who gave the order for the driver to take them knew he was drunk, but said to take them anyway.

Chris was also going through a messy break-up in his marriage at the same time. All that came to a head one day, some weeks after the crash. He had split from his wife and had been forced to sleep in his car because his commanding officer wouldn't let him move into staff quarters. His wife wouldn't let him see his children and he had become very depressed. It ended up with him attempting suicide in the basement of the flats where his wife was living.

Things had been good for a while once we had got together, but now everything seemed to be getting to him. I suppose once a soldier is out in Civvie Street life is very different, they are suddenly on their own, having to make their own decisions and if anything goes wrong it is down to them to sort it. At first it's great, they can please themselves when they get up in the morning and if they don't feel like having a shave, they don't have to, but after a while insecurity sets in.

The army doesn't prepare the men for this and when it hits them it's a huge shock. In Chris's case this was even more so, because he had joined up very young at only eighteen and he hadn't really known much of the world outside the army. I knew Chris was tired; he was working very hard and long hours. And at the same time my health was also going downhill fast.

Chris's ex-wife had also been causing so much trouble for him and making his life hell. She seemed to want to bleed him for everything she could, and as I've already said, things didn't get much better for a long time with her running up debts and Chris having to pay them off.

In early 2002 Chris's depression was becoming much worse. He didn't want to get out of bed in the mornings and he had serious mood swings. It was as if he was angry with himself, but he didn't know why. He would be all right one minute and then – bang! – he would throw something and be slamming doors. It became so bad that he had to give up work.

The doctor put it down to depression due to his leaving the army and his world being so different. He would just stare into space all day and had very little to say to me. I was so worried because this wasn't like the Chris I knew. He had always been so happy and smiling and now he was a virtual recluse, shut away in his own world.

Most nights he would have nightmares and he would jump up out of bed and fly at the window, pulling the curtains down. He would be pretending to shoot at something or someone outside and he would roll around on the bedroom floor like he was in combat.

It wasn't long before things got even worse and he wanted to commit suicide. Some nights he would take himself off out of the house and be gone for hours on end, never saying where he was going. I used to be worried sick. He had also started to collect all sorts of different weapons, knives and swords and other really freaky objects; he had shelves full of them. He had become obsessed with buying them.

The first time he attempted suicide at home was scary. He had been pacing up and down and crying uncontrollably saying he wanted to go, he'd had enough. I had an idea all that day that something wasn't right.

He picked up a large Samurai sword that was as sharp as hell and was holding at his throat. I was screaming at him to put it down, I tried to phone for help, but he ripped the phone out of my hands. He had locked the doors and I was panicking like mad, screaming and swearing at him. I had never seen him like this before and was actually beginning to believe that he was turning into a monster. My legs were like jelly.

In the end I climbed out of a window and ran across the road to Tina's house to use their phone. I rang the police and in no time we had armed response police all over the place because he had a weapon. Luckily it ended peacefully, but they took Chris away and he was taken to Chorley Hospital.

They kept Chris in hospital for two weeks. They didn't have to section him because he was by this time compliant with the doctors and he eventually agreed to stay with them voluntarily. I went to the hospital every day to see him, but there were times when he didn't want to speak to me and this really upset me.

I began to question myself and ask what I had done to this wonderfully once happy man to make him like this. I was putting huge pressure on myself, I was finding it very hard to cope and I was blaming myself for what was happening to him. I was devastated; our world seemed to be falling apart.

Things didn't get any better and when he came home he was just the same, often begging me to let him go. He would stand in front of me crying and laughing at the same time, and he would be talking to God. He was still going out of the house at night and staying out for ages, never telling me where he was going, and he would never tell me where he'd been.

I was convinced this wasn't just depression. I'd suffered from depression and I knew this was more than ordinary depression. I suspected it was something to do with his time in the army and I wrote to The British Legion. They said I should contact the army direct so I began writing to the army. I wrote to his commanding officer in Germany, and I wrote to London. I sent letters all over the place to anywhere and anyone who I thought might be able to help.

I explained about Chris's condition and insisted that what was happening to him wasn't normal depression. It had to be something to do with his time in the army. I told them that I thought it had begun with his accident in the Land Rover and his commanding officer's refusal to help him then. What I could understand, but they couldn't, was that here was a man who had known nothing else but being looked after, firstly by his mum up to the age of eighteen, and then by the army. He had never been in a position where he hadn't had a routine in his life. To me there was a huge lack of care here for this man and I said that the army should have looked after him better, both while he was in there and afterwards.

I remember his mum telling me that when he had told her he was joining the army she had laughed at him and said he wouldn't last five minutes. He set out to prove her wrong, so much so that when he first joined the army his mum had told him to let her know that he was OK and settled, but he didn't get in touch and he'd been gone for weeks doing his training while his mum had heard nothing.

So she set off and went over to his camp. I couldn't believe it that the army had let them in to see him – two Irish women turning up at the gates of a British army camp and they just said, 'Yes, come in, we'll go and get him for you.' I asked her what she had done to those guards on the gates. After all there was still some trouble going on with the Irish and certain terrorist cells over there. She told me she hadn't heard from him in weeks and she was going to find out where he was and if he was all right.

Chris had set out to prove his mother wrong and had done just that. He loved the army, it was his life and suddenly to be without all the routine and daily organisation had obviously hit him hard.

I had letters back from the army's top brass apologising, but saying that it was nothing to do with them because he was no longer in the army. It felt as if they had used him and then washed their hands of him. I thought they had something to answer for and I wasn't going to let it go.

Then all of a sudden I had one letter from a Captain that was different. He said there was nothing he could do, because Chris was no longer in the army's care, but he sent me an address of a place he thought might be able to help. A place called 'Combat Stress' which was at Audley Court in Newport, Shropshire.

I wrote to them and they said they would send for him to assess him, but this was going to take twelve months. During those twelve months we went through hell. Chris's condition got much worse with him again trying to kill himself.

One night he drank a bottle of brandy and downed lots of pills. He was laid on his bed in full army uniform waiting to die. I rang the ambulance and the police. They came, but couldn't do anything because he told them he didn't want any help. They stayed with us and told me they would have to wait until he collapsed and then they could treat him because he wouldn't be in a fit state to object.

So for ages that night the police were traipsing around following Chris up and down the house waiting for him to drop. The ambulance was parked at the end of the street also waiting. It got to almost morning and the policeman said, 'C'mon Chris, this has gone on long enough, we don't want to have to wait for you to collapse, if we have to, we will section you.' In the end Chris agreed and went with them and boy, was I relieved. The worry and the stress that I was going through was unbearable.

After that night there were others, and every time he went out I was on tenterhooks. There were times when he would wander off and not come back for days on end. I would ring the police and they even had the police helicopter out looking for him. Then he would turn up, but he would never say where he'd been. There was another time when he was outside cutting the grass. It was a lovely day and I had been trying to cheer him up, telling him that I loved him and trying to get him to smile.

I had gone upstairs to hoover the bedrooms and I was having problems with the Hoover when Hayley came in. I asked her to go down and ask her to ask Chris to come up and have a look at it for me. She came back saying he wasn't there. I told her he was outside cutting the grass. She came back saying she couldn't find him, but something odd was happening; there was smoke coming out of the garage.

When I went down and tried to open the garage door, but couldn't. I was banging on the door and screaming for him to open the door. I rang the police and they broke in to find him sat in the corner with a bottle of brandy and the place full of petrol fumes. I was shaking, I was a right mess. He was taken away again. Later when I looked in the garage, there was a noose hanging from the rafters.

Chris's time in hospital was not good. He was treated as someone who was suffering from depression, but at the time they didn't know that it was worse than that and to make it worse he was in there with some guys who were acting like they were soldiers. This really wound Chris up. There was one guy who believed he was ex-SAS and he'd even had a tattoo on him that was SAS, but he had never even seen service. It was things like this that Chris couldn't handle and he wanted to thump them.

When I would go and visit him in there he would say to me that I should let him go, and that he didn't want to live. There was no bloody way I was letting him go and I told him in no uncertain terms that we would get through this.

Eventually in 2003, when Chris was sent for by Combat Stress, he finally went to Audley Court in Shropshire. It was a huge house that resembled a mansion rather than a hospital. They are the Ex-Service Mental Welfare Society. It is a private organisation, but the army pay for any treatment that can be attributed to anything that they might have caused, and all treatment including any medication is paid for by the army. They also sort out any money including war pensions that the ex-servicemen might be entitled to.

It is a place where ex-servicemen go for treatment for Post-Traumatic Stress Disorder (PTSD). Chris was admitted for two weeks for assessment and it was confirmed that he was suffering from PTSD. If Chris had been found to be suffering with this while he had been in the army, he would have been sent to them straight away. The army treat service personnel there who have been affected by situations in a war zone.

What I haven't mentioned was, I was also very ill around this time. I had been going to see my doctor for a while; but not getting any better. My problems were very similar to Chris's, but caused by far different reasons. Chris's problems had outweighed mine; I'd tried to put my own health to one side with worrying about Chris and whether he might kill himself. I had this lovely man who had made me so happy and had made me feel safe for the first time. Yet here he was in such a state that he didn't want to live any more.

Was I to blame? I asked myself this over and over again. Had I contributed to him feeling the way that he did?

In the time since we'd moved back from Ireland and settled in Leyland I had piled lots of weight on and had become very tired and unable to look after myself. I had lost all energy; I couldn't even bathe myself, make a meal or look after my children and Chris properly. I had always been the sort of person who would be up first – happy and smiling and getting everyone organised, but I think everything had become too much and I was suffering from overload. I had been fighting to keep life for Chris as stress-free as I could, but it was as if Chris's problems were telling my brain to be on guard. It felt like I was unsafe again, although I knew Chris would never harm me in any way.

There was never any doubt about my love for Chris. I adored him and if anything my love for him was stronger than ever, because I wanted him to be safe and I would do anything to make sure he was safe. Then one morning, it all became too much for me. I couldn't get out of bed and I had never been like that before. That was the start of me being really ill.

When I could get up, I would come down in the mornings and just lie on the settee unable to do anything. The kids must have wondered what the hell was happening in their world. Chris would get up and take them to school and then come home and do everything around the house. I could see he was worried about me and that was just adding to his stress, but there was nothing I could do, I was so ill.

My doctor referred me to the Chorley and South Ribble Domestic Abuse Counselling Service (DACS) in July 2002 but it soon became clear that I couldn't cope with this level of counselling, so I was referred to the Westfield Mental Health Team.

I was having to have carers come in to help me bathe and to help with the house and look after the children and Chris. We had had a stair lift put in because I couldn't even make it up the stairs under my own steam. On top of all that, I had a serious bowel problem that had been there for a long time, but up until then, I'd ignored it.

I suppose I thought not going to the toilet for weeks on end was normal for me, I just sort of accepted it as a way of life, but the pain was now getting much worse. When I did go to the loo I was struggling to go so much that I was tearing myself. I had to go to see my doctor. The doctor already knew about my other problems. All this and having to worry about Chris as well was really taking its toll.

I was so ill that I was convinced I had something really seriously wrong with me. The first thing that goes through your mind is 'Cancer' and although my doctor had tried to convince me it wasn't that, I really believed that it was, and that he was wrong.

My depression was eventually diagnosed as Post-Traumatic Stress Disorder, brought on because of all the violence I'd suffered during my marriage to Blake. The doctors and psychiatrists had also said that my childhood had played a part as well – the childhood abuse by my neighbour and the bullying from other kids as well as my dad leaving had all played a part.

But it was the violence in my marriage that had tipped me over the edge. Then Chris being ill had brought it all to a head again. I was feeling that my world was falling apart. To make matters ten times worse, I found out that Blake was back in the area. I had known that he was out of the army and living with a girl in Preston, but then I heard he'd broken up with her because he'd been arrested and had been given community service for beating her up, but now he was out, and had moved back to live with his mother whose house was only just further up the estate.

Unfortunately there was nothing recorded on his army records or with the police about what he'd done to me, otherwise he would have gone to jail for what he did to her. The only evidence was my medical records. But he did go to jail for offences against others. He was given a three-year sentence, but only served eight months for good behaviour.

Chris was at home most of the time, but he did have to keep going back to Audley Court every so often for his treatment, and when he was away I was scared stiff that Blake would come around. Then one day I looked out of my window and there he was, standing across the road from our house just staring at my windows; I could have died.

Straight away I rang the Domestic Violence Officer who I'd been in touch with when I lived at Robin Hey. She came round and I was a nervous wreck. She said there was nothing she could do unless he actually set foot on my land. She could see the state I was in and again suggested I get some counselling. I had CCTV fitted and had to see my doctor because I was suffering from severe panic attacks and palpitations. It made it worse knowing about his recent serious convictions. I believed he must have been getting desperate.

Chris and I decided to get ourselves a dog for a bit of added protection for when he was away at Audley Court, so we bought ourselves a German Shepherd called Gemma. We later bought another one called Samson, but that was two years later.

As well as the problems with Chris and with Blake coming back on the scene, I also had the bowel problem to contend with (Severe Bowel Dysfunction) This was becoming one of my main concerns at the time, mainly because of the pain I was in. I'd had problems with constipation from being small, but now it was becoming unbearable. I suspected the anal rape along with all the stress contributed to it getting worse.

My doctor sent me to see a specialist at the Royal Preston Hospital. I had also been diagnosed as suffering from osteoarthritis as well as having an irregular heartbeat, and for this I was sent to Chorley Hospital to see a Consultant Cardiologist who said I had a mitral valve prolapse and regurgitation.

There just seemed to be one thing after another and all this illness, both Chris's and my own appeared to make matters worse. I would try to be upbeat as best I could for Chris's sake, but we were both so down at this time. I knew I had to try to appear to be in a happy mood to lift Chris, but it was hard work. There were a lot of days when I was so ill that the last thing I had on my mind was wanting to pretend that all was well.

2002 had been an awful year. Chris had tried to kill himself numerous times and had gone missing every other day. The most worrying time was when he disappeared for two solid days. I had contacted the police because I was so worried. I was sure they would find him dead. They had everyone out searching – even the police helicopter.

They asked if I had any idea where he might have gone, and the only thing I could think of was that he might have gone to find his children. I gave the police the address I had for his ex-wife which was in Scotland and they contacted her to see if she'd seen anything of him, but she hadn't (they'd been divorced since September 2000). Then after two days he came back, but he wouldn't say where he'd been and I didn't push him on it.

But it did make me more determined to try to get Chris access to his kids. I knew this must have been a contributing factor to the way he was feeling. I contacted Social Services who advised me to get in touch with a mediation body called Cafcass. After weeks of trying to find Chris's ex-wife, they finally tracked her down; she had now moved to Cumbria and had a new man in her life.

It was bad enough her keeping the children away from Chris, but now she had taken things a step too far. She had changed the children's names, giving them her maiden name. She also changed their first names. She had done this because she wanted them to have names that resembled her partner's.

She hadn't asked Chris's permission and by doing this she had broken the law. You can only change the names of your children if you are given permission, if your ex-partner has died or if they have been out of their lives for five years and not wanted anything to do with them for that length of time; but this wasn't the case here and Chris was furious.

We arranged with Cafcass to organise a meeting between Chris and his children and a date was set. This was around Easter 2004. They had to meet in a room in the County Hall across from the courts building. Chris was still suffering from his PTSD problems and the anxiety of all this was making him sweat buckets. He was worried, but excited at the same time.

The assessor from Cafcass had pre-warned us that he thought Chris's ex-wife had probably put ideas into the kids' heads about their dad and it was obvious during that meeting that she was manipulating the whole show. They were already pretty worked up and she made them worse by holding them both on her knee and saying to the Cafcass assessor, 'There is no way he is ever seeing my kids on his own.'

Chris had taken Easter eggs for the children, but she had made the situation so tense and the kids were so worked up that she eventually rushed them out of the back door of the court and Chris didn't even get the chance to give them their eggs.

I had waited across the road in the car during the time they were having the meeting. We had decided it might be for the best, but before we left; the assessor from Cafcass told us that he had spoken to Chris's son before the meeting and he had come out with something that was the sort of language you would only expect an adult to use. He had said about his dad, 'He is only a sperm donor, James is my dad.' This naturally upset Chris, but the assessor assured him that his mother must have planted that in his mind; it just wasn't the sort of comment a kid would use. The assessor said he couldn't believe the way she was. He said even he had felt intimidated and found her very hard to deal with. He said he thought she was a loud woman and that her attitude stank.

Chris wanted to leave it at that and was ready to admit defeat, but there was no way I would let her win; we'd come this far and we weren't giving up now. We arranged further meetings and more court hearings took place, but Chris's ex didn't turn up for any of them except the last one.

At that meeting the judge told her that she'd had plenty of opportunities to put her case forward, but had not bothered so he told us that he was making an order that Chris could see his children under supervision with a view to him seeing them on his own at a later point.

A date was set, but as usual she didn't turn up with the children, so we had to go back to court. There had been reports prepared before we all went before the judge. In his address, he said he had given careful consideration to everything. He pointed out that Chris's ex had broken the court order and for that, he could send her to prison, but he said he didn't feel that would be of any benefit, and it would only cause distress to the children.

She told the court that there was no law that could make her let him see her children. The judge said that while he felt Chris should have access, it was obvious that she was going to be noncompliant and short of jailing her there was nothing we could do about it. It looked like she had won, and Chris felt he'd done as much as he could.

This was all happening around 2003–2004, and the stress of it all had made me even more ill as well as Chris. I was by now getting much worse and was sometimes visiting my doctor twice a week. He was convinced my problems were down to stress, but I felt there was something much more seriously wrong with me. Every day was a struggle to do the simplest of tasks. I was convinced I had cancer; I had all the pain from my bowel problem, my bones ached all the time, the palpitations in my heart … I just couldn't cope!

I had told him all about the violence in my first marriage, including the incident with the petrol, and the rape. I explained that Blake was back in the area and that I'd had to take some extreme measures to feel safe, such as getting the dog and installing CCTV. And I told him just how it had all affected me. I began to think that he was fed up with hearing me moan about things, but I knew how ill

I felt and wanted something doing about it.

So, I went to see another doctor and explained it all again to him. He decided that I should see a specialist at Wrightington Hospital, which I did and it was there that I was diagnosed with osteoarthritis and prolapsed discs. From there I was sent for physio and hydrotherapy treatment to Chorley Hospital.

I went along and got into the pool. The water was lovely and warm and very relaxing, but I hadn't been in for very long and I was struggling to do what they wanted me to do. I told them I couldn't lift my leg and one of the women in charge said, 'OK, Jeanette needs to come out.'

So I started to make my way up the sloping steps out of the pool, but as I was going up the steps and the water was no longer supporting my weight, I just slumped to the floor. Before I knew it they had me out on the side drying me off and covering me in talcum powder. Then they sat me down with a cup of hot chocolate; I felt like a right spanner.

I remember looking at all these other ladies who were much older than me and I wondered what they must be thinking of me. I was so worn out from that short, but very relaxing session that I soon felt myself nodding off.

I was also still suffering with severe constipation and it was getting worse. I hadn't been to the toilet for about six weeks at this point. I paid another visit to my doctor with this problem. He examined me, and feeling all around my belly, he could tell that I had a very compacted bowel. He gave me some strong laxatives and told me to take the whole bottle of the stuff he'd given me during the course of that day. He said if I couldn't shift it I would end up having to go to hospital to have it sorted out.

Luckily I did move it, but I ended up tearing myself in the process. After that I just visited my local chemist and bought over the counter laxatives – horrible chocolate-flavoured stuff that was pretty revolting, but it did the trick for a while. I was more concerned with other things that were going on; such as what was happening to Chris.

He was still having his problems, he was still going down to Audley Court and although by 2004 he was showing some signs of improvement, he was a long way from where he needed to be and he would still go wandering off, causing me to worry like mad.

As the months wore on my bowel condition seemed to get worse and I had to go back to the doctor again. This time he referred me to a specialist at Chorley Hospital. I had tests done including a colonoscopy. I was told I was a very complicated case and sent for further tests to Manchester, to St Mary's Hospital. There I had more tests including one where they insert balloons inside and inflate them to give you the sensation of wanting to go to the loo. They told me afterwards that I'd had three of the things inside me before I felt any sensation at all.

It showed just how relaxed and stretched my bowel had become. I was told then that I was suffering from problems with my sphincter. This is the muscle that opens the bowels, enabling them to function. Following that, I was sent to Wythenshawe Hospital where I had even more tests.

The test I had done at Wythenshawe was a barium meal test. The solution was inserted inside me and then I had to sit on a machine that was a bit like toilet, but was in fact a camera. I then had to try to move my muscles and part with all this stuff they had bunged me up with. This was so they could see what was happening and measure whatever it was I parted with, but I couldn't.

The nurse said to me that I was one of the oddest cases they'd ever come across. They had never had to send a patient home with the barium meal still inside them. They had to ring the doctor and ask him what to do. He said I would have to take laxatives and they sent me home with loads of the stuff in the hope that some of it would work. The doctor warned them that if I didn't part with it, it would just harden and harden. And it did, it took me weeks to get rid of it all!

Following that, I was given more laxatives and enema solutions to help me keep in control, but none of those actually solved the problem and I was then sent to Bury to a Bowel and Bladder Incontinence clinic, where I was seen by two ladies who were fantastic with me. They did lots of tests and had me doing exercises to help me to build up the muscles in my back passage, but after doing the tests they found that I was getting minuses on a lot of the tests.

They came to the conclusion that I might end up having to have a colostomy bag fitted. But they said they would do more tests because I was so young and didn't want to end up with this. So it was decided to try a different kind of physiotherapy whereby Chris was brought in and had to be shown how to help massage my bowel to help make me go.

They showed him how to find my bowel and how to massage it round to bring it to where it was supposed to be. He was absolutely petrified; he was so scared of hurting me, because it was quite a painful process. I was hoping that by doing this it would return to normal and I wouldn't need the colostomy, but it didn't and I was again referred back to St Mary's.

He knew I didn't want the colostomy and he said there was a new pioneering treatment that was just coming out. It was something that he had been developing, but at that moment it was all in the trial stages. I told him I was prepared to give it a go. The procedure involved running a wire down my spine to my sacral nerve and attaching it inside my body; then I had a box on the outside that controlled it. The best way I can describe it is, it was a bit like a Tens machine. They could turn it up or down. On the first attempt they turned it up eventually to 10 and they thought I would be jumping through hoops, but I could only just feel it at that.

The operation to connect it all up was done at Wythenshawe Hospital and I wore it on one side of my spine for two weeks. They then decided to move it over and try it on the other side. That side was better as I did have more feeling there, but it still wasn't strong enough to be doing any good.

The doctors did consider running two wires down my spine with one wire running to each of my Sacral nerves, and placing a box with a battery deep inside the cheek of my bottom that would be operated by remote control. This would operate rather like a pacemaker does for the heart and I would have had to go back every so often to have the batteries changed.

This went on for a long time. They were developing a new system whereby they ran the wires through your nose and down the gullet and connected to both sides. They seemed to think that might be a more direct route and that it might work better. But that was a long way down the line from where we were in 2004 and I was glad about that, as I certainly didn't fancy having that done.

The years that I had suffered with this problem were down to my brain being concerned with other issues. I would be so wrapped up in everything else that my brain was pushing to the back of my mind the need to go to the toilet and there were times when I hadn't been for weeks, but when I did eventually go, the pain was so bad and I would literally tear myself because I was so compacted. I often sat on the toilet and thought I needed to get an ambulance.

Luckily I didn't have to go through with that new procedure because, by some miracle or other, a couple of years later my bowel began to work normally, but more about that later.

12

2005–2006:
finally getting to grips

By 2005 things were starting to get better for me. I had again been to see my doctor and I had also been back to DACs for counselling; they passed me on to the Westfield Mental Health Team and it was after I'd had a session with my counsellor there that I woke up one morning and suddenly had a feeling like a huge concrete block had been lifted off me. We've all heard the saying 'A weight has been lifted off my shoulders'. Well, that is just how it felt.

A lot of things seemed to come together all at once; it began with the visit to my doctor. I remember that day we had a very frank discussion about my problems and he'd said to me 'Jeanette, the problems you have are both physical and mental, but if you are going to get anywhere near to sorting them out, you need to sort your head out first. Do that and you might stand a chance.'

I left his surgery that morning and at first I was angry – convinced he was wrong; I was sure there was something physical wrong with me, but the more I thought about his words, the more I wondered if he might be right. Then when I awoke that morning with all those good feelings inside me, I believed he probably was right and it was such a good feeling that I never wanted to lose it.

I had already started to chase the army for justice for Chris back in 2002. The British Legion had been wonderful and had helped me with contact addresses. It was a man called James Bond at the Legion who had helped me to get the ball rolling. He had put us in touch with a firm of solicitors by the name of TSS Law in London who started by helping us to get legal aid. That was around the end of 2002. By 2004 we had moved on and now had a hell of a fight on our hands with the solicitors and the army passing reports to and fro, but at least we were getting somewhere.

I was also beginning to feel that I was getting somewhere too, after the turning point of that session with the counsellor and the feeling that my burden had lifted. It was the start of getting justice for all the crimes that Blake committed against me. But I was still suffering from all my physical ailments such as bowel dysfunction, heart condition, spine condition and osteoarthritis, and I was later to find out that I had a brain condition too.

By the end of 2005 though, I had started to have driving lessons. These went on for quite some time. I was enjoying them and also enjoying my newfound confidence. Chris seemed to be improving all the time too, although he was a long way off being better. He still had days when he was really down, but seeing me feeling better helped him and me seeing him smile again helped me to be more upbeat, so we sort of bounced off each other.

My driving lessons went on; I took my test, but failed. I was driving down near the docks in Preston when the examiner told me to stop the car. I immediately slammed the brakes on, thinking he wanted me to do an emergency stop, but all he wanted me to do was to pull over in a safe manner.

I took it again and failed again. I was ready to give up, but Chris wouldn't let me; he convinced me that I had come this far and that it would be silly to stop now. I began to book blocks of lessons in the hope that it might help. I took my test again and I failed again. I was definitely ready for packing it in, but again Chris talked me round and I took it again, and this time I passed. I came home and tried to look miserable as if I'd failed again, but I couldn't keep my face straight and Chris could tell, I was so overjoyed at passing.

My life really seemed to be taking off. I had always wanted to join the police. Ever since I was a little girl I'd loved the idea of wearing a uniform and the black and white was for me. I thought that if I could have joined the police I could have helped people who had problems like mine, but I realised that my health conditions could prevent me from joining any of the services.

I had looked at other options and had seen a college course on criminology. I thought if I could do a course like that, it would give me a bit of a head start. The course was being run at Preston College and I enrolled. I started the course in September 2006 and I loved it.

Soon I was getting assignments and I needed a computer. My friend Tina who lived across the road got me started and taught me how to use one. I was busy writing away, but getting all these red and green squiggly lines appearing. Tina told me they were all down to spelling and grammar mistakes. She showed me how to check them and correct them. I was over the moon when all these options came up and I soon found out that I could write as well as anyone else with the help of this wonderful spell-check facility.

My tutor at college was great, she knew all about the problems I'd had in my life and would often ask me how things were going. She helped me to grow in confidence. I was soon asking questions and getting involved in discussions. I couldn't believe it: here was little old me, who had been useless at school, mixing with all these clever people and holding my own with them.

I would come home and I would be analysing everyone. I was beginning to pity some of the criminals I was studying because I could understand that they had done what they had because they had major issues of their own – be it drugs or broken homes or whatever. Chris used to laugh at me and ask me why I was analysing all these people, but I couldn't help it, and apart from that, it helped me to understand why people did the things they did. It also helped me to understand what had happened to me and to become even stronger and more confident as a result.

I was at this time doing a small cleaning job. I had joined a cleaning agency at Walton-le-Dale called CPL. They had offered me a few extra hours a week and I was placed at a company called Eric Wrights at Walton Summit. I had passed my test and was driving to work in our old Ford Mondeo; some of the other girls had cars too and we used to take turns at sharing cars.

While I was at Eric Wrights I was asked if I would like to help out at one of their events days. They were due to have some bigwigs come along for a day and they needed people to wait on them at lunch and to serve tea and coffee. I agreed to help; I had to dress in a nice skirt and white blouse.

I was as nervous as hell. I had to go around with a huge teapot offering them more tea or coffee. I had visions of spilling the tea all over them. I came out and was shaking, but I was told I had done really well and that they had all said they loved me in there.

By now we had our own computer and Chris had been on it looking at cars for sale. Our old Mondeo was getting tired and Chris wanted me to have a nice car as a reward for all the hard work I was putting in at college and with my cleaning job.

He had seen a nice Hyundai Coupe for sale, a really sporty car. We'd saved up and it was going cheap, so we thought, why not? The car was in Newcastle. We decided that my stepdad Mark should come with us to collect it.

The idea was that we would all go up, Chris would drive one car back and Mark would drive the other back, but it didn't go according to plan, and nearly ended up with Mark getting in trouble.

We had stopped to ask for directions and when we were about to set off again, Chris was directing my stepdad and as he was setting off I shouted at him not to go yet, but he did, he set off and crashed the Mondeo into a bus. The door was hanging off and the mirror was gone. My stepdad shouldn't even have been driving the car because he wasn't insured for it so we had to say his name was Thomas Badger, which is Chris's first name. We admitted responsibility for the accident and told the bus company to let us have the bill and we would pay it.

We eventually got to the guy's house where we were buying the Hyundai and he felt really bad that we'd travelled all that way up there to buy his car and ruined ours in the process. Our Mondeo was in such a mess that we couldn't drive it back, so the guy agreed to get it sorted out for us, and let us know when it was ready. What a day! All that way to get this nice sports car and we ended up like that.

I loved that car and it was soon my pride and joy. It was white with a black leather interior and Chris had even bought me a private number plate that read: S3XY. He said it spelt 'Sexy'. I carried on working at Eric Wrights and taking it in turns to run the girls to work. One night I was driving home with the girls in the car and we were all chattering away merrily and I suddenly felt a bump. It was quite a low car and I said to one of the girls, 'What was that?' She laughed and said 'You've just gone over the bloody roundabout instead of going round it.'

'I thought the car felt funny – a bit lopsided, I wondered what that was', I said. I didn't feel it go up, but I felt the bump as it came off.

They all thought it was hilarious, and I had to laugh too. I could imagine me going round the roundabout with two wheels on the road and two on the roundabout. Luckily I hadn't done any damage, which was a wonder because it was quite a low car.

Not long after that I moved to another cleaning contract company called Solar and I was sent to do some cleaning work for a company called Datrix where I got on well with the bosses. I was also poached by a guy who had a Portacabin on the same site. He knew I was a cleaner and he asked me if I would do a one-off cleaning job for him, cleaning his cabin, so I agreed. He paid me £25 for a couple of hours' work.

I decided to put that £25 in a separate jar. I had been quietly thinking for some time about starting my own business and I looked on that as being the first money I'd ever earned as a self-employed person; even though it was only a one-off. But the more I thought about it, the more it seemed like a good idea.

I was getting on well with the other cleaners that I was working with, but the boss of the contract cleaning company was a nasty piece of work; he just used to look down his nose at you, like you were something off the bottom of his shoe. And I had put up with enough crap in my life without taking it from him too.

I was still doing my college work and enjoying that, but I knew that if I was to start on my own I would have to learn a lot more than criminology. I had seen how these cleaning companies had operated and how important it was to have things like Health and Safety records up to date and risk assessments in place, and I would need to be clued up on first aid and a lot of other things as well.

But I had this newfound confidence and Chris was also improving and was always ready to back me up, and that felt good. I also had it in my mind that if I could get things going, it might give Chris a boost and that he might slowly become involved and get back to working again. He hadn't worked now for quite a while, and to be honest, he was still virtually unemployable at that time, and it wasn't likely that someone would take him on as he was, but he felt he was ready to start to do something, even if it was only a little at first.

We had talked it over and gone through all the pros and cons and I decided to go to speak to Datrix and tell them that I was considering leaving to start my own cleaning business. They said that if I left, I had to contact them right away. They said they didn't want to lose me and asked me if I would give them a price for doing their cleaning. They said if I wasn't going to be with Solar then they would come to me.

I decided to get Christmas out of the way and then see how I felt about it. It was a big step, but one that excited me.

13

Meeting my dad again

Towards the end of 2006, around the time I was thinking about starting working for myself, there was one night when Chris and I had sat down in the evening after I'd come in from my cleaning job, I'd turned to Chris and out of the blue I asked him if he thought my nan might still be alive; my dad's mum.

He asked me if I wanted to find out, so I said I'd just like to know. I knew she had lived somewhere in the Huyton area of Liverpool. So one day we set off to Liverpool and headed for Huyton. We turned right at some lights and stopped the car, there was a man walking towards us so we decided to ask him if we were in Huyton.

'Yes you are, and if I were you, I'd keep going otherwise if you stop for too long somebody will have the wheels off that car … it's that bad round here, you don't come to Huyton with a flash car like that', he said.

'Oh, right', I replied, not knowing if he was joking or serious.

We turned the car round and went in the opposite direction. I don't know if it was my stupid psychic weird stuff coming out of me. I told Chris I remembered going to my nan's as a little girl and I could remember some high-rise flats being near to where she lived, but I was only about two the last time I came here. We drove around for a bit then I said to Chris to stop the car.

'I'll go and knock on that door and see if anyone knows of her around here.'

I knocked on the first door I came to and I couldn't believe it. It was Nan's house and it was her who opened the door. It was so weird. When I introduced myself to her, she called us both in and we had a good natter. She looked quite young, much younger than I'd expected and she was a really bubbly woman, full of life.

I asked her if she knew where my dad was, but she told me she hadn't seen or heard from him for over twenty years, the same as me. She said the last time she had heard anything about my dad was when he'd been to visit her son, my dad's half-brother.

She said it was so sad because my Nan told me that her mum – his gran, had died two years earlier at the age of a hundred. And she had waited and waited for her grandson to call and see her, but he never did.

We chatted for a good hour and I told her that I hadn't been well and what had happened in my life. We exchanged phone numbers and she promised me if she heard from my dad or if she got to know where he was she would let me know. She showed me a photo of my dad; it was quite a dark old Polaroid picture, and before leaving we agreed to stay in touch and meet up again soon for a coffee.

It must have been a good two months later, around February time. Chris was out in the garden with the dog and he had his airgun with him. He was taking pot-shots at a target that he'd set up. My Uncle Ralph had called and was asking Chris if he could have a go. Silly really, because my uncle ended up with a black eye and a cut on his nose after the gun kicked back and smacked him in the face.

When Chris and me had stopped laughing, he suddenly told me that there was a message on the phone for me. He told me after that he hadn't known how to tell me.

'I think you'd better go and listen to it', he said.

I went to the phone and dialled 1571 to listen to the

message. It was a man's voice, a very soft quiet voice that spoke – 'Hiya, it's your dad. Give us a ring when you're free, here's my number. I'm in the area, maybe we could meet up?' and that was it. My heart was thumping, I went outside to tell Chris, but Chris already knew. He said he had already spoken to him and that he'd rung back specially to leave a message for me.

He'd told Chris that he had been to see his mum and she had told him that I had been there not long before. She gave him my address and telephone number and told him I was trying to find him. Apparently his girlfriend had said that he had got up one day and said he wanted to go and find his mates, and on the way up he decided to call and see his mum. She'd told him about me.

I wrote down the number from the phone message and it took me until the evening to pluck up the courage to go and ring him, but even then I didn't do it from home. I went down to the phone box at the bottom of the road; I didn't want to do it at home. I was shaking like a leaf when I dialled the number and when he answered I was so overcome that we hardly said much, because I was blubbing so much. I just couldn't stop crying; then he said, 'Right, I'll have to go now, I'll give you a ring tomorrow'. I didn't realise right away, but he didn't like people crying.

The following day he rang back and this time I was OK. He asked if I wanted to meet him. I told him I did, but I was absolutely scared to death. He said to meet him down Leyland Lane. Chris drove me down in our beautiful posh new car. He said he would be in a Mini. I got out of my car and was looking for him. I saw this Mini and I was looking round for him when I heard him shout 'Net' which was what he had always called me.

I didn't know what to think. There was this short baldheaded man standing in front of me, smiling at me. I had always had this vision in my mind of my dad as being tall and with a mass of black curly hair. And I'd always thought that if I ever saw him again after all those years I would run into his arms and it would be so lovely. But here was this man who I didn't recognise.

It felt really hard, but I didn't cry. He drove me to the Jarvis Hotel which is where he was staying and we walked round the gardens having a good natter, but every time I looked at him he was a complete stranger to me. Definitely not the man I remembered as a child. It felt really awkward to me; I couldn't feel the emotional bond that I thought would be there. I couldn't understand why I wasn't really upset after all those years.

I kept thinking: this man's a liar; he's not my dad, because I could not see any resemblance whatsoever to the only memory I had of him which was from the one picture I had of us all at the Leyland Festival with his curly hair, and the one my Nan had shown me two months before was of him but with short dark hair. I had kept that image in my mind all those years, and there was no way I could connect this man with my dad in those pictures.

I did eventually realise that twenty-two years had passed and people do change, but the change to my dad and the way I had remembered him from all those years ago was massive. We had a good talk and he told me everything that had happened to him over the years since he left.

My dad's mum had put my dad and his younger brother, Andrew up for adoption when they were both little because she couldn't cope. They grew up in a Barnado's home, and a number of foster homes. Their gran was not happy about this, but there was nothing she could do about it at the time. She had done what she could for the boys and kept putting money aside for them for when they grew up.

When they were sixteen and about to go out into the world, his gran met him and gave him the money she'd saved. He said it was the first time he had ever felt like somebody cared.

But even having that bit of money hadn't stopped him from getting into trouble. He spent time in borstal. He had a lot of issues of his own to deal with. I suspect a lot of them were down to the insecurity he'd had as he grew up in different homes and without any proper family to love him.

His mum would never talk about what had happened, but as far as I could gather she'd had an affair with an American serviceman who was stationed over here and when it came time for him to go back, he just upped and left. She was left on her own with no money and no means of support. She had no option, she felt, but to give her boys up for adoption. As heartbreaking as it was for her, that is what she had to do.

That night my dad came round to our house to meet Chris and the kids, but shortly afterwards I noticed Chris was beginning to go downhill again. I had always spoken very highly about my dad to Chris. I had always put my dad on a pedestal and Chris got it into his head that my dad would think that he wasn't good enough for his daughter.

I think Chris had probably thought that I might never see my dad again and now that I had, he felt like he was second-best. It became so bad that it contributed to another suicide attempt. I had tried to explain to Chris that I didn't have the emotional attachment to my dad that I thought I would have had after not seeing him for all those years, but it didn't seem to make any difference to the way Chris thought my dad saw him.

Chris had it in his mind that my dad would say 'This man is no good for you' and I would take his word for it. I tried to explain to him I certainly didn't feel that way and that I would never do that to him.

But my dad did have those feelings for me. He did still see me as his little girl, he was on the phone to me about ten blooming times a day and that didn't help Chris's situation. He was finding it very hard to cope with me having this new man in my life.

As time went on and my business was developing, it was very hard, and I felt as if my dad was pushing me to do certain things. In his way he was just trying to guide me, but I felt like I was being pushed into things that I wasn't ready for.

He kept telling me to take on more staff. 'You need more staff, take on more staff.' He wanted me to go bigger quicker, but I wasn't ready for that. OK, I was busy and working hard, but that was me and the way I wanted to be at that time. So I didn't listen to him and he started to get a bit funny with me.

It got so bad that it was causing arguments between him and his wife. They'd had a fall out, and one night she rang me up and had a right go at me. I found out later that she was finding it very hard to accept that my dad all of a sudden had this new family; she'd had him all to herself for all those years and now I was in his life and he was showering me with all this attention so I suppose it was jealousy or insecurity, but I can understand how she must have felt; Chris was feeling just the same.

I also found out later from her that my dad had been in a right state after him and my mum had broken up and when he couldn't see me. He had been in prison and had come out to end up living rough. He had slashed his wrists and had been in the paper for trying to kill himself by jumping off Preston bus station, and all this was because he missed me so much. My mum had known about this, but had hidden the papers from me.

When my brother Milton found out that dad was around, he said he didn't want to see him at first. He said if he saw him, he would kill him, and my dad also said that he didn't feel the time was right to see Milton just yet, so it didn't happen right away. But when they did finally meet, they were fine with one another.

Then my dad started telling me that I should be doing this and that for my brother and that didn't help our relationship. I didn't need my dad telling me what I should be doing for Milton. I had worked very hard for what I had, and I didn't see why I should be giving it to my brother.

My dad was feeling sorry for Milton, having finally realised he truly was his son (they looked very alike now). He wanted to help him and gave him a job; he was even living with Dad and getting everything he wanted. Dad thought I should be doing the same. I would never see Milton stuck and I would help him when he needed help, but I wasn't going to give him what I had worked so hard for. Dad told me that I was being cruel and horrible.

Milton was a Jack the Lad, he had been involved with drugs. I had lent him money and never got it back, but my dad said I shouldn't be lending him the money; I should be giving it to him because I had it and he hadn't. My dad saw me as being quite nasty for being like that.

Milton and I had always been close because of the connection with my dad and I had a sort of psychic connection with him, for example, there was one night when I couldn't sleep. I had got up and was agitated about something, and then I saw flashing blue lights go past my window. I immediately felt it was something to do with Milton. I slipped my coat on and went over to his house and there he was with blood pouring from his head. He'd been drinking and had been attacked while walking home. He didn't want to go to the hospital, but I made him.

So we did have a very close relationship, but my dad thought I should do lots more for him. I did what I thought was fair but if he wanted my success, I was of the mind that he should work for it, like I had done, and stop playing around, but Dad couldn't see it that way and he let me know in no uncertain terms.

His wife told me that he had found it very hard to cope at times and it had been her who had looked after him through all those bad times. She felt that because I was doing so well, he was now putting me on a pedestal and she felt threatened by my success and she was worried that he wasn't going to be there for her as much.

In the end my dad wrote me an absolutely awful letter saying that I was too big for my boots, etc. It was so cruel and horrible that it was the only time I cried.

'Am I really like that?' I asked Chris.

'No you're not', he told me.

'Well why is he saying that then?'

'Because he doesn't know you, that's why', Chris said.

In the end I drove myself off to a car park on Woodlea Road and sat there for ages listening to my music. I remember a song by Pink that I played over and over, it was a song with words that really summed up everything I was feeling at the time. I sat there and cried my eyes out.

And there was another song, a Mariah Carey song that had words that went, 'You can do what you want to me, but it's not going to work' and although these songs made me cry, they made me realise that I needed to move forward. I took them as a positive sign and thought to myself, all those years I'd worried about him and wondered if he was OK. I'd even wondered if he was still alive. Well if he couldn't accept me for the way I was, I didn't care. I had Chris and he was all I wanted and needed, I couldn't want for anything more. I had seen my dad now and I knew he was safe and well.

I didn't know if seeing him was going to be a permanent thing or not, but it looked like it hadn't worked out and it was time for me to move on. I wasn't going to let that affect my life any more. I was going to move forward.

I didn't see my dad after that for a long time. In fact it was probably a couple of years later. He went back down south to where he lived and had his own business, which was a building firm. Milton did keep in touch and they get on very well to this day. The next time I saw him, I did take more notice of his appearance and it was his nose that stood out a mile – I remembered it, and I also noticed that he did in fact have some hair although it was only on the sides of his head and it was grey now instead of black.

Meeting my dad came at a time when Chris and I had been fighting a lot of other battles with our own health and we were now trying to sort out my daughter Emma. I suppose having all this going on and my dad suddenly turning up out of the blue had added more pressure all round. I was really wound up with a lot of concerns at the time.

Emma had had hearing tests done in 2006, but they hadn't showed anything out of the ordinary. Then I think in August 2008, Chris's mum came over for a while and stayed. She loved coming over for the Illuminations at Blackpool. One morning she asked me if I'd noticed anything odd about Emma's behaviour. She said she wondered if Emma might have a hearing problem.

'No, she's always like that, she's just got selective hearing', I said to her.

But Chris's mum was adamant there was something wrong. I spent the next couple of months monitoring Emma and watching her sneakily to see if Chris's mum was right and as soon as I was completely satisfied that there was a problem I made an appointment to speak to Emma's teacher at school.

I was sure that if I could see something wasn't right then surely they must have noticed too, but I found it strange that they hadn't said anything. When I did speak to Emma's teacher, she told me she had had some concerns about Emma's behaviour and had wondered whether there might be a problem with her hearing. She said she was going to speak to me about her in due course. She suggested I take her to see our GP.

Our doctor was a bit hesitant about it; he said it was

probably something she would grow out of. I wasn't so sure so I went back to the school and saw the school nurse. She arranged for Emma to have some speech and language tests done with the educational psychologist. These did confirm there were problems with her reading and spelling, and from there Emma went on to have far more indepth tests done.

The early psychological tests involved talking about Emma's early life to see if there had been anything that might have happened that could have affected the way she was and of course this was very upsetting for me. The psychologist did say that early events in her life would have played a part.

I had to go through everything that had happened in my marriage to Blake and virtually relive everything again. I had to tell them how I used to have to make sure Emma was shut away in her bedroom for hours on end because I didn't want her caught up in our fights.

I explained to them how he resented Emma, but loved Hayley to bits and how he would push Emma away. I felt in those days that it was safer for Emma if she was in her bed by the time he came home from work, but this meant she was alone in her room for long periods at a time.

I began to question myself – had I caused all these problems? I had to relive seeing my beautiful little girl sitting on her bed rocking and then holding her arms up to me whenever I went into her room. Had I played a part in the way she was now? I didn't know but I knew that if I hadn't protected her in the way I did at that time, his resentment was so strong that I honestly believed he could have seriously injured Emma, maybe even have killed her.

All these feelings of guilt washed over me time and again for months afterwards and I was in danger of drifting back to the way I had been, but Chris kept me strong and I suppose I had so many other things happening in my life at the same time that I was lucky in a way.

Having already met with the educational psychologist and not being satisfied with his assessment I decided to take it further and applied for a full meeting with the County Council, teachers and all the other specialists. I believed that Emma should be statemented.

At that meeting the teachers really wound me up, saying things like 'We don't see any of this that you are talking about ...' and so on. They were suggesting there might be issues at home that were causing Emma to behave the way she was. I stood up and said 'Stuff you all, I've had enough of this!' I was really at breaking point by this time.

But not long after that meeting, Emma did something that caused me to return to my doctor and he arranged another meeting with Social Services and Emma was given an initial assessment by a social worker. Emma had tried to stick a pin into Carrie's eye: she said she wanted to see if it would pop, she had also tried to set fire to her sister's hair and to cut off her sister's finger with a pair of pliers. None of these things were done out of anger, but just out of curiosity to see what happened when you did things like that.

Emma had that first assessment at Balfour Court and then went on to have many more over the following months. There were a number of doctors and psychiatrists assessing Emma for different reasons, but the main one was a Consultant Child and Adolescent Psychiatrist. They were the Child and Adolescent Mental Health Services (CAMHS) based at Shawbrook House in Leyland.

Emma had lots of tests done for all manner of things and each doctor who was responsible for that individual check did his or her own report. The Speech and Language Therapist said in her report that Emma had some communication difficulties that suggested she might have Autistic Spectrum Disorder. All these reports were all then put together and they eventually agreed that Emma should be statemented.

14

Working for myself

In January 2007 I had left Solar and started working for myself. Datrix asked how much I would charge them. I quoted them £400 per month. I was silly really, but I'd based my figures on the job being two hours a day, and five days a week equalling ten hours per week, and I was charging £10 per hour. That made it a total of £400 for a four-week month.

I thought because I had only been earning just over £5 per hour at Solar, that I was quids in. I hadn't allowed for everything else such as chemicals, transport, equipment and everything else that goes with running your own business. I also had to take course after course to learn about various aspects of managing your own business and the courses all had to be paid for at college.

The £25 I had saved in the jar from cleaning the guy's cabin paid for my mops and buckets and dusters etc. I was lucky in that Datrix already had a vacuum cleaner that I could use, but I did buy a new one with my first month's pay, because theirs was useless.

I hadn't been there for long when the firm next door asked me if I would do their cleaning for them too. They were a company called Force Travel. I quoted them the same as Datrix and soon I was earning £800 per month. Then their accountant, who had an office next door, asked me if I would clean for her for just a couple of hours a fortnight. She was really nice and later on I began to use her as my accountant.

I was still doing my criminology course as well and it wasn't too long before I had my head in my hands thinking, 'I'm gonna break down, I can't do this'. I would come in from work and Chris would be asleep on the settee. I began to resent this although I didn't say anything at the time. I had a feeling that Chris was feeling left out with me doing all this work and my college courses too, and one night my fears were confirmed.

Chris was becoming withdrawn again, and it was as I had said earlier, partly because my dad had come back on the scene. One night he had taken himself off in the car and had been gone for hours. I became more and more worried as the night wore on so I called the police; I knew something was wrong.

The police were out searching for him; I had given them a description of the car and told them about Chris's history and his suicide attempts. Later that night the police came back and said they had found him in the car on Moss Side industrial estate miles from anywhere with a hosepipe through the window. He was unconscious, and in a bad way. They had taken him to hospital with a police escort. I was panicking, but there was nothing I could do.

I went to see him the following morning. I couldn't go right away because I couldn't leave the children. When I saw him, I couldn't believe it; he looked awful. The nurses were taking blood samples from him every hour and checking him and he was on oxygen. He slept for a whole week.

I was told he was a very lucky man, because for one thing, where he was; he was lucky to have been found at all. Secondly, because he was so far gone when they found him, he was almost gone, he had almost died. When he did wake up his eyes were so glazed, he looked awful. I cried my eyes out.

I just kept asking myself, 'What am I doing to him, what is the problem?' and all I could think of was that this was my fault. I had become so wrapped up in everything I was doing that I'd ignored things that were going on at home.

The day afterwards the police had the car brought back to me. It was such a mess. I couldn't look at it at first, but when I did eventually go out to see it, it was unbelievable. It had black seats but everywhere else was black too. It stank of smoke and petrol fumes. There was no way I would ever drive that car again. I hated it and after I'd had it completely valeted, I sold it. I was lucky because I got what I had paid for it.

When Chris was allowed home he had to have his counsellor visit him. He had been seeing a guy called Bob, but Bob had just retired around this time so it was a new bloke that came out. His name was Jim, a Scottish man. He was very nice and Chris soon got to know him and got on really well with him.

Jim also had a lot of kind reassuring words for me too. He said he was very proud of me for the way I'd stuck by Chris, and he understood how difficult it must have been for me having to go through all this. For many months after, I spent hours talking to Chris trying to reassure him that everything I was doing was for our future; for him, me and the children. Eventually, quite a long time later, he told me what had made him do what he'd done. He told me that he had been feeling worthless. He said he could see me doing well and he thought he was holding me back. He thought I would be better off without him. Of course, I put him right on that and told him so in no uncertain terms.

After that, and once Chris had spent some time recovering, I started to take him to jobs with me. Just getting him to drive me there at first – I didn't want him to become too involved too soon. I knew he wouldn't be able to handle the stress so he would take me and then sit in the car reading or listening to the football on the radio.

Then one day I'd been given a job in Bradford. The council had asked me if I could cover it for two weeks while someone was off. I told Chris that I didn't know how I was going to cope with it. I was on my own at the time. Straight away Chris said he would do it. I was a bit worried at first because it meant him leaving home at 4 o'clock in the morning to get there and I didn't know if he was up to it. He had helped me with one or two bits of jobs, but nothing like this and so far away.

But I could see he was really up for it so I agreed and he took it on. After he'd been going for a while I could see there was a slight improvement in him and although he was shattered he seemed to be enjoying doing it, it gave him a sense of purpose and he was becoming much more talkative.

I had got a new vehicle by this time, a pick-up truck, a Mazda BT50. It was a much bigger car than I'd ever had before, but I felt it suited the job and was ideal for the business. The business had been growing steadily, but we were coping. I hadn't taken any wages from the business at this point.

I know it might sound strange because after all you usually go out to work to earn money, but I had been ploughing it all back into the business at that time. I needed to have that backing behind me, ready for anything that might come up.

One day I'd gone to a nursery in Euxton to price a job. The lady there had known me from my time with the contract cleaning company. While I was there, a guy turned up who worked for Lancashire County Council. The woman from the nursery told him who I was and why I was there. She said I was a fantastic cleaner and that I had come to give her a price.

'Oh! Give us your card, I work for ground cleaning support services and I might be able to put some work your way', he said to me.

When I got home I told Chris what he'd said but we both felt that nothing would come of it. I left it and didn't bother chasing him. Then after a few weeks I had a phone call from him asking to meet me at a place in Hapton near Burnley. He gave me a time to meet him there. Chris drove me and waited outside in the car. I went off to my meeting dressed all smart in my skirt and blouse and my high heels. I had my hair done and my make-up on. I wanted to impress.

When I got there, I found it to be nothing much more than a building site and he wanted me to start cleaning right away. I had thought that he was just going to show me what the job was and that was all. It was lucky that I was in the pick-up and I had all the cleaning stuff with me (mop, buckets and brushes etc.) I'd taken it all along ready to set the job up if he had wanted us to start.

So there I was cleaning these stairwells. It was all really dusty and filthy, and there was me, looking a right sight in my tight skirt and high heels. The lads on the site were having a right good look; I felt so embarrassed. All this time Chris was fast asleep in the car.

When I got home, Chris and me had a long talk about things. Up till then I had been on my own apart from the odd time Chris had helped, but we were managing. I still had Datrix and Force Travel and I also had the nursery and an accountants round the corner, but now with this coming along I was wondering how I could manage.

We decided to take on an extra member of staff, so I took one woman on and she covered Datrix and Force Travel and I did the nursery and the accountants and the council stuff. After a while Chris said he would cover Hapton because it was a building site and more of a job for a bloke than a woman. We were quite lucky because we had that contract for some time and we would have had it much longer but for the LCC restructuring and taking all their cleaning work in-house.

There was another funny situation where the area officer from LCC had asked me to go over to Accrington to St Mary Magdalene's school to have a trial clean. I went over and got stuck in, but I could soon see that this was such a huge school. I called the supervisor over and said, 'Oh my God, am I expected to clean the whole of this school?'

'No, we only want you to clean one room, we just want to see what you can do in a school', he said.

By this time I had already cleaned three rooms. He thought it was fantastic and we got the contract. As time went on that year we got more and more work offered to us, which meant we had to take on even more staff and before we knew it we had about four cleaners working for us. I was going on different courses learning about the different aspects of business management, including accountancy, but I soon found that it was taking up too much of my time so I put that work out and got an accountant.

It was the same with the Health and Safety. I had passed my level 2 qualification, but I decided to farm that side of things out to a company too. I went on courses for business enterprise, which highlighted how businesses fail and I was adamant that wasn't going to be me; I wasn't going to go down any of those roads. I had so much on my mind that I would lie awake half the night thinking about work. I would get up and go into the office to write something down in case I forgot.

Then I learnt about wine! I found that a glass of wine in the evening helped me to relax and soon I was sleeping like a baby. Don't take that the wrong way! I was only having the odd glass now and again, mainly on Friday nights to help me to relax and enjoy the weekend. One of the courses I took with the Business Enterprise people was all about switching off and unwinding, and it is so true, you do need to separate your work from the rest of your life. But it really isn't that easy when you are the boss!

We had done far better than I had imagined when I'd first started the business just one year earlier, and all the extra work had come by word of mouth; we hadn't advertised for work at all. The staff I had all lived near to the jobs and they were all good people.

As time moved on we had found ourselves doing really well. In the first few months from January 2007 to April 2007, I had made £745 profit, but I hadn't taken a wage out of the business. All the money had gone towards buying new equipment. Because we were getting more sites to clean we needed more equipment and it was also at the back of my mind that I needed to be sure there was money in place at any time should we need it.

By the time we had reached March 2008 we had a very different business. Our accountant had called us in and told us that we needed to become a limited company and to register for VAT. She said we had gone way past the threshold of £67,000 that we were allowed as a sole trader. We had turned over a huge £92,000 in the first year.

I remember when I got my first cheque from LCC it was for £10,000. I had never seen that sort of money in my life before, but now I seem to receive cheques for £2,000 every other day and it doesn't bother me. I don't look on it as being my money; it is just business. I think it is because I was determined from the very start that I wouldn't let myself be overawed by it all. I had never taken a wage for myself for a long time, and I always made sure the money was in the bank for when it was needed.

My accountant started to explain how it all worked. She told me that I had to sell over my company to my new limited company. She wanted me to put the company goodwill value at £50,000 – she explained this wasn't 'real money' as such, but on paper only, the value of my old business. I couldn't grasp this at first and said 'No way, I don't want to sell it'. I had worked for that money and I wasn't selling to some fictional company. She explained that I was only selling my company's goodwill. Only on paper was there any money changing hands.

I said, 'Well there is still £34,000 outstanding that is profit, so I should be allowed to keep that because the tax man says it's what I've earned; is that right?'

'Yes', she replied.

I was up until then a sole trader and that money was in my account. I said to her

'Give me my £34k and I'll give you £7,000 to put into the bank account of the new limited company. That will mean then that the limited company 'in theory' owes me £57,000 … right?' She agreed.

It took me a long time to grasp everything that was happening. I now had to deal with VAT and people paying me VAT. I was asking myself why I had to be involved with VAT all of a sudden, and there were other taxes to deal with such as Corporation tax. I'd never had any dealings with stuff like this so I handed all that side of things over to my accountant. We were still struggling to get on top of Chris's, and my PTSD.

I was still pretty weak and tired some days, and I was still working very hard on the cleaning. Just because I was managing director of a company didn't mean I sat in the office all day, and when I say 'office' I mean the spare bedroom – it's still the office to this day. I was out there getting my hands dirty every day and doing the invoices and the paperwork at night or at the weekend.

By this time, April 2008, we were employing seven members of staff. A lot of the work we had was only temporary jobs until we got in with LCC properly, and then it became a case of taking on an extra pair of hands as a casual, then another and another. Then we would make someone permanent.

Chris of course could see how the business was growing

and wanted to become even more involved. I was wary of putting too much pressure on him at first, because I didn't want him getting stressed and his health going backwards. Although he was still vulnerable, he seemed happy to take more on, and it was good to have him involved; it brought us even closer together.

We could see that it made sense to bring Chris in as an employee and put him on the books as one. It would have been difficult for Chris to find a job at that time because of his illness and even if he'd got an interview he would more than likely have been turned down as he was obviously mentally ill, and rejection could well have set his recovery back even further, but I wanted him working with me anyway so it was a win-win situation. He was still not sleeping properly at night and this made him very tired during the day.

One weekend in October 2008, we'd done a job over Burnley way at a place called Oakenhead Resources Centre for disabled people. The following Monday morning, I got a phone call from them asking if I could go over and drop their keys off.

It was half term school holidays and I asked Chris if he wanted to come, or did he want to stay there with Carrie. I even offered to take Carrie with me if he wanted to have a lie down, but he said he would stay and that I should leave Carrie with him.

I set off for Oakenhead in my lovely Mazda. I really enjoyed driving that car, it was so high up, I could see everywhere. I got over to Oakenhead and dropped off the keys then set off back home. My mind was on getting back to Chris, we had hardly spent any time together and because it was the holidays, it meant we had the rest of the day to ourselves.

I had got back onto the M65 at Junction 8. It was a horrible wet morning. I was told later that it was what was known as a microclimate, where in a small area there was s a huge amount of water put down in a short space of time. I had been overtaking in the fast lane and indicated to pull back into the middle lane. There was a lorry in the slow lane and he just pulled out into the middle lane at the same time as I was moving over. I braked hard, but with all the surface water I just aquaplaned and spun across the nearside lane, across the Junction 7 slip road, hit the barrier, knocked down a lamp-post, overturned and went down a steep embankment and into a tree.

It all happened so fast, but I can remember as I was spinning around and the car overturned, I was pushing my hands against the side of the car frame inside. If I hadn't pushed myself away from the side window I am sure I would have been thrown out and my head would have been taken clean off. I don't know what gave me the presence of mind to do what I did; it's weird! It is surprising what goes through your mind in situations like that. I remember doing that and then as the car tipped, I hit the roof and then it hit the tree. I was dazed and sort of half out of it, but as I was coming round I could hear a hissing sound and see smoke and I could hear people shouting, 'There's a woman in the car, she must be dead. I can't see her or hear anything.'

All these voices and I can hear all this; I was really dizzy. And I could see Carrie's coat in the car, but because I was so dazed I couldn't remember if I'd had Carrie with me. We had lots of big tins of paint in the car at the time and although they had been in the back section of the pick-up, they had flown through the windows and come straight through the cab of the car and out through the front window – right past my head!

It is strange how many thoughts go through your head in such a short space of time. I was thinking the car was going to set on fire and I remember wondering why the airbags hadn't gone off, but at the same time glad they hadn't, because I thought they would have knocked me out. All these thought are just flashes that happen so incredibly fast.

I managed to scramble out of a window and I could feel a bit of a sharp pricking pain in my chest. I was trying to scramble up this really steep embankment, but because it was so wet and I was so weak; I just kept on sliding back down again. I don't think I'd been there long, but by the time I'd got out of the car, the fire brigade had arrived and the air ambulance was on the scene overhead. There was a lot of panic going on. I was trying to shout for help, but nothing would come out.

Eventually three or four firemen came down on ropes and got to me. They were asking me how I was and if I had any pain. I told them about the pain in my chest. They wrapped me in foil blankets and they wanted to put me on a small stretcher. I didn't want them to do that, I felt stupid and even with all this happening, I was worried that I would look silly going up the hill on that thing.

Eventually they decided that it might be better just to try to walk me up the hill with them using the ropes and whatever trees we could to stabilise ourselves on the way up. So that is what we did. Once at the top, I was put into the ambulance. Once in the ambulance I was shaking like mad. They asked me about family and if they could contact anyone. We found my phone and they rang Chris, but didn't manage to speak to him, he missed the call. They left a message on his voicemail telling him what had happened and that I was being taken to hospital.

The accident had happened at Junction 7. And they were taking me to the Royal Blackburn Hospital. On the way to the hospital the pain got a lot worse and the paramedic said that was because the adrenaline was wearing down, he said he suspected I had broken my ribs. By the time we had reached the hospital, Chris had already got there from Leyland. He had heard the voice message and was panicking. He had been imagining all sorts of things being wrong with me; or even finding me dead.

I was X-rayed, but they couldn't find any broken bones. I thought 'Thank God for that', as all I could think about was getting home – I had work to go to and I didn't want to let people down or Chris either, but Chris was having none of it and the doctor said, 'No you can't go home, you've had a nasty accident and we need to keep you in for observation'.

I said there was no chance – I wasn't staying there! I told him to give me a paper and I would sign myself out and that's what I did. But on the way home, my breathing was hurting; the pain was bad.

'Right, I'm going to cover the jobs that you'd normally do. I don't know what time I'll get done, but will you be all right on your own?' Chris asked.

That night Chris went out and did all the work that I should have done. My mum took the girls to give me a chance to rest, but poor Chris didn't get home until nearly midnight that night. The day after that, I insisted on going back to work. Chris argued with me saying I couldn't go back, it was too soon, but I was adamant that I was going, and I went, but I was in so much pain that I ended up back in Casualty.

I was X-rayed again and found to have three broken ribs. I contacted the Royal Blackburn and asked why they hadn't found them. The hospital said it wasn't unusual for them not to have found them at the time of the accident because of swelling and bruising. But even if they had known, they would have treated me exactly the same because there is nothing they can do for broken ribs apart from rest. My concern was, if I'd known I had broken ribs, I wouldn't have taken the risk of going out to work and possibly puncturing my lung.

It was then that Chris's role in the business started to take off even more. He seemed to come out of himself and it was obvious he wanted to be more involved. Up until then I'd tried to keep him away from all the stress of the business, but now he wanted to play a part. I think it hit him that he could have lost me that day and it made him think.

He also said he thought we should think about getting married.

'About bloody time', I said.

I had asked him years earlier one leap year but nothing had happened. Mind you, we had both been through a really bad patch that had lasted for about five years or more. Now we were both feeling better and things were looking much better all round – apart from the crash!

It is surprising how a crash like that can open your eyes, a close to death experience makes you realise that you need to do more here and now, and not to waste a moment. It made Chris and me realise how much we meant to each other.

It took me a long time to get over that crash. I did take a bit of a back seat for a while until I was feeling better, but it wasn't for long because that wasn't me! I don't like resting for too long, it reminds me of being ill. I had got to the stage where I knew how my brain worked and I knew if I sat around for too long, I would start to go back to the dark times. If I wasn't careful, I could easily allow my brain to get back into its old ways of imagining that things weren't right, and I was in danger of being ill all over again.

I had learned to have the presence of mind to know that I need to keep myself busy and focus on what is important now and not to worry about what might be. It has been a constant battle to stay well, but I know it is my work, my family and above all, Chris that ensures that I carry on having positive thoughts.

I didn't want to drive for a while after that either; it took me some time to get my nerve back, so Chris took more control in that direction and would run me to the jobs. Chris said to me, 'Do you know Jeanette, I'm actually enjoying this, we're getting out together and it's good.' He was happy because we were doing things together, going to jobs and meetings together and it really made him feel like he belonged. He steadily took more control of certain areas of the business and it was good to see him so happy again.

We had to find a replacement car – and quickly. Chris had seen an old Ford Mondeo on the estate that was for sale for £250, so we bought that and used that for a bit. It was only a runaround. We had been using my mum's car again until we managed to get this one. For the money we paid for it, it certainly did a good job for us. It ran well and didn't let us down once.

Following the accident Chris officially became an employee of the company around the end of 2008. I had a primary school in Hoghton that was looking for a supervisor. It was only for an hour and a half a day, but I felt this was perfect for Chris. He started and absolutely loved it and they loved him too. As well as doing the cleaning they had him doing bits of maintenance work which suited him down to the ground. He was the only man in the school and they would call on him.

'Chris, I've got a shelf that's broken, can you sort it for me?' or a cupboard door had fallen off.

He has always liked DIY and the more they found for him to do the more he enjoyed it. He's still working there today, they won't have anyone else. They know all about his history, but they love him; he has such great skills and does all sorts for them.

But at that time, even I wasn't unbreakable and I had to constantly remind myself not to allow my thoughts to drift back to the bad times. It would have been so easy to just sit back and take it easy, but I knew that if I did that, I was on a slippery slope. The business kept me busy and in a way I found it to be very therapeutic. It stimulated my brain and I found it easier to remind myself that it was better to work hard and have those good feelings than to sit back and let things get the better of me.

I surprised myself sometimes, because I knew I had to fight every day to keep going. There were some nights when I would only be getting home at around 10 p.m. And don't forget; we still had three children that needed looking after as well!

But we managed and things grew at a steady pace. We continued to be offered more business and by 2009 we were being offered contract work, which meant more financial security because we knew we were guaranteed the work and this meant we could take on extra staff knowing their jobs were sound.

By the end of the second financial year, April 2009, we had turned over around £180,000 for that year; this was double the first year's turnover, but our overall profit margin was less because I had now started to take a wage, albeit a small one, but I was also taking a fuel allowance. It had been getting to the point where I was out of pocket by driving around to all the jobs. I had to run some staff about and deliver cleaning products and equipment, and some of our contracts were many miles away. My accountant suggested I start claiming for the fuel, as it had been costing me out of my own pocket for so long, so I did.

I couldn't believe that we were doing so well. I found it hard to understand how we were achieving it all. It was obvious it was the schools work that had got me to where I was and that got me wondering what I could do to give something back. We had by now given up the cleaning for Datrix and Force Travel. The schools work had become far more important and worthwhile.

People were always saying to me how they couldn't believe how I had turned my life around and they kept asking me 'What's next?' The only aim I'd had up until now was to keep improving. I kept setting myself targets and sometimes my accountant would say I'd never achieve them, but I always did.

I remember her asking me when I first started out, what I hoped to achieve in my first year and I told her £20,000 would be amazing. I had passed that easily. I just kept setting myself a target for each tax year and wanted to keep doubling up and doing well. She would say to me, 'Why do you need to do that? You're doing really well. Why can you not be happy with what you've got?', but I would say, 'No, I'm doing it', and off I'd go, and every time I'd prove her wrong; I'd smash my targets. I would sometimes get a bit giddy and think to myself, 'Well, what next?'

Chris and I had reached a point where we were both feeling the best we had felt for a long time and the subject of our getting married had come up again. I decided I wanted a June wedding, but it was now November and that didn't leave much time. But Chris knew that once I set my mind on something it would take a mountain to stop me, so I set about making the arrangements.

15

Getting married again

With the business now doing so well we now had a good bit of spare money in the bank, something I'd never had much of before. I was also happier than I'd ever been in my life so I decided I was going to have the wedding of a lifetime, one that Chris and I deserved; after all we'd both overcome so much and we had waited for long enough.

In November 2008 I set about making the arrangements without involving Chris at all. Again, this was me trying to protect Chris from all the pressure and stress. I was going to sort out the lot and I intended that we would have nothing but the best. I booked a top hotel as the venue; it was the De Vere Hotel at Blackpool, a superb setting right beside a golf course.

This was something I did involve Chris in; this and a meeting with the wedding planner to sort out the table plan, but apart from those two things I hardly involved Chris at all. We booked the De Vere in the November and by Christmas I had sorted out the dresses. I had decided I was going to have all my girls as bridesmaids and my best friend Susan who worked for me as my chief bridesmaid. I had set myself a colour theme of red and white.

My own dress was from a local shop, and as soon as I saw it I loved it. I had never seen a dress like it and I haven't seen one as nice as it since. It was white with red and it was laced up the back. It cost me a fortune, but I loved that dress and I knew it was just what I wanted.

The next few months were mad. I just kept adding things to my list of what I wanted. I organised a water feature for underneath the wedding cake and a huge 'bomb' above the dance floor that would explode and shower everyone with goodies as they were dancing. I planned for hundreds of balloons to be released on the lawn outside the hotel after the wedding.

There was of course the photographer to sort out and I wanted lots of ad-lib pictures to be taken as well as the official photographs. And I booked the flowers with a lady from Fleetwood and I had to go all the way over to her farm to meet with her and describe exactly what I wanted. I asked her for tiny crystals to be inserted into each flower, and all the flowers were to be red and white roses.

We had made arrangements that Chris would spend the night before the wedding at the De Vere along with his dad and all the rest of his relatives from Ireland, apart from his mum and her granddaughter. They were going to stay here with me at our house.

On the day of the wedding I was due to arrive at the De Vere in a horse and carriage, and the bridesmaids would arrive before me in a car. That just left Chris to sort out. I didn't want him to feel as if it was me getting all the attention, so I arranged for a Rolls Royce to collect him from the hotel after breakfast and take him to have his haircut and shave, it was then going to take him to Blackpool airport and he would be brought back to the hotel by helicopter.

I spent countless hours phoning people making various arrangements and checking that everything was right and in place. I was convinced that something was bound to go wrong; I'd organised and booked so many different things that something was bound to happen.

It was only a couple of weeks away from the wedding when I'd come up with the idea of the helicopter for Chris.

I managed to find a firm that hired helicopters out, but it was down to me to find a pilot to fly the bloody thing.

Blackpool airport had given me a list of names of pilots who were freelance and I began ringing round them all. By the end of the list I was begging, but eventually I got lucky and the flight was on. I even booked a company to do a fly-past with a plane towing a banner that said, 'Congratulations Mr & Mrs Badger. Married today 6-6-09'.

I was leaving nothing out; this was going to be the wedding of a lifetime – it was the wedding of our lifetime and it was going to be a day to remember.

The room for the wedding was beautiful: all the tables were decorated with flowers and small gifts for the guests on every table. I had organised the music and had booked a karaoke along with the disco for the night. That was a treat for me, because I like singing and I wanted to sing at our reception.

The day before our wedding arrived and it was more stressful than I had ever imagined it could be. All Chris's relatives arrived from Ireland. Most of them were staying the night over in Blackpool at the De Vere. They had hired cars from the airport so there was only Chris and one or two others to run over there.

I knew our house would be hectic that night because we had so many people staying that night. I eventually got back from the De Vere at around 8 o'clock. Everyone was round at my mum's house when I got back. Mum and Mark had the barbecue going. I should have been eating with them, but I'd already eaten with Chris and his lot at the hotel, but I didn't tell mum that; I told her that I was too nervous to eat.

When we finally got to our house around half past nine or later, we had to bath all the kids that night and get them settled. That in itself was a major battle. Then there was Emma who didn't like all these people around her and

..adn't seen her cousin from Ireland for ages so they were busy catching up and not listening to anything I said. I also had Chris's mum staying at ours, my brother Milton and his girlfriend Kelly – they were both legless after being at the barbecue for hours and drinking too much. Their kids were also staying and so were Susan and her husband, so the house was packed and all the adults were pie-eyed apart from Chris's mum.

Kelly was a hairdresser and specialised in all sorts of fancy styles, she decided to have a practice at doing the kids' hair for morning and finally gave up about midnight and went to bed. Susan stayed up with me until 2 a.m., but then made her excuses and took herself off, leaving me on my own.

I hadn't slept the night before and I didn't sleep that night either. I spent nearly all night trying to sort my hair out! I was trying to get my hair extensions in place and I had the straighteners on it, in fact I'd used the straighteners so much it is a wonder I had any hair left. I had even burnt my ear when I got it caught in the straightener. In the end I thought, sod it!

By daybreak I was so tired, I was having hallucinations due to two nights without sleep. The night did seem to go quite quickly though and when Susan came downstairs at about 9 a.m. and said my hair looked OK that was a relief, because I hadn't any energy left to mess with it any more.

The kids started to get up and were running about like headless chickens. None of them wanted to have their hair done and I was fast losing my patience with them all.

I was also beginning to convince myself that Chris wouldn't turn up. I had visions of him off around Blackpool on his stag night and I had begun thinking that I wasn't good enough for him.

The night before the wedding I had a printout done for Chris telling him of all the arrangements for the following morning. I put down where he had to be at certain times and the sequence of events. Then I got a phone call from him. 'Jeanette, where is it I'm going to have my shave and haircut done?' I was blazing, I had given him that in writing and all he had to do was follow the list, but he'd lost it. As if I hadn't enough to do!

The florist had sent the flowers to my house, but hadn't attached the crystals to the flowers so we had to start doing that, and what a painstaking job that was. One tiny crystal had to be stuck to each red flower. My bouquet alone had about fifty of them on it. They were on very small pins and it took us ages, but they looked fabulous when we'd done them.

I had Milton's girlfriend, Kelly here; she'd come to do everyone's hair, but she was very laid back while I was panicking and feeling like something was going to go wrong, and I felt like there was only me bothered about anything. The kids were all playing up and messing about and I was losing my rag with them. Emma was in a mood and she didn't want to be bothered with any of it.

Eventually, however, everything seemed to come together until the girl came to do my make-up. I'd got all the kids sorted out and had put my own dress on. I was always led to believe that it was supposed to be me who was the one who got pampered.

The make-up artist was shocked to see me with my dress on. 'Oh! You've got your dress on ... you shouldn't have your dress on yet!'

She was worried about getting make-up all over my lovely white dress. Well, I didn't know that, did I? I ended up with a huge towel wrapped around me having my make-up put on. All I could think was; what could go wrong next?

The weather had turned out to be horrible too. The day before was glorious sunshine, but on my special day it was raining. But there was no way was I going to let a few spots of rain spoil this day. I was determined – we had come this far and been through so much.

By the time it came to leave for Blackpool, everyone had arrived at our house. It was standing room only with every corner filled with people. Thirty people including my neighbours, and mum's neighbours Mr and Mrs Sharples were even there.

I had arranged for a coach to take all the guests from our end over to the De Vere and I was going on the coach with them so far. The coach driver came in, looked at me and said, 'Wow, what a beautiful bride!'

I said, 'Get away with you', but he kept saying what a lucky lad Chris was. Then it was time for me to get on the coach and the heavens had opened. The driver got a huge brolly from the coach and he put down loads of towels on the floor so I wouldn't get my dress dirty. He was a real star and looked after me that day.

All the way over to Blackpool I was watching the weather and praying for it to pick up, but the nearer we got to Blackpool the wetter it seemed to get. I was hoping that it would clear up before we got there. A lot of the things I had planned were for outdoors and I was praying for everything to go right.

The plan was that I would meet the horses and carriage near to Stanley Park and the coach would take the rest of the party on. We did get to Stanley Park a bit early and we had to wait. We waited and waited but there was no sign of the horses and carriage. I tried to ring the firm up who was doing it, but there was no answer.

I was supposed to get there at roughly the same time as Chris was to land in the helicopter. He was only flying from Blackpool airport and was supposed to land on the golf course on a lawn in front of the bar. He should have been landing on the car park, but they wouldn't let him so we changed it and got permission from the golf club to land on the lawn which was right in front of the suite at the hotel where we were having our wedding ... Perfect!

Well it would have been if the horses and carriage had been there. Everyone was looking at me and could see how upset I was becoming. I was about to give up and tell the coach driver to take me into the hotel when around the corner it came, followed by the Rolls Royce for the bridesmaids. It was a beautiful coach, all cream with gold trim and there were four gorgeous Palomino horses pulling it.

We were about half an hour late by this time. Not late for the wedding, but late for the time I had in my mind to arrive at the hotel. The coachman said I had given him the wrong time.

It was still raining, the coachmen were holding umbrellas and everyone helped to get me into the coach with my stepdad holding my dress off the floor as I got in. The bridesmaids got into the Rolls and they went off before us. Everyone was shouting and cheering. And as we set off we could see a helicopter flying overhead and I wondered if it was Chris.

We set off and even though the cover was over the top, the sides were open and it was freezing. I had hoped it was going to be a part of the whole proceedings that I would have been able to enjoy, but I was so cold all I could think of was getting there as quickly as possible. I hadn't realised how long it would take for the horses to get us there and we were a little bit late. But you can't make horses go any faster than they can go in those conditions. Chris had been there a bit when I arrived. And the pictures prove it: there are some of him in the bar before the wedding! He told me later that he'd had a wonderful morning. He had been picked up in a Rolls, had a flight in a helicopter which had taken him and his dad right over Blackpool, round the Tower and then landed back at the hotel, and to cap it all when he got to the hotel there was a guy there who buffed his shoes up after he'd walked across the lawn.

When I arrived the coachman pulled in round the roundabout and up to the front of the suite. The photographer met us and said we were now quite pushed for time, saying 'We need to get a move on. I'll get a few poses of you in the carriage and then we need to get you up there.'

I just said 'Well there is no way I am bloody rushing.' I had paid a lot of money for my day and I wasn't being rushed. It was something I wanted to enjoy.

We got there and went up the red carpet and I had left instructions for everyone to be inside when I got there, but they were all outside, so I said I wasn't getting out until they were all indoors. So they all went in and we had some pictures taken in the foyer. While this was happening I heard my music come on, it was Shania Twain's 'From This Moment On', and straight away I thought my tears were starting; I had to tell myself to pull myself together.

I walked down towards the front with my stepdad Mark who was giving me away. As we were walking I could hear people gasping and commenting on how beautiful my dress looked. I was more worried about how my hair looked with having done it myself, but everybody had told me it looked amazing. I got there to the front and the registrar started, 'I would like to welcome you all here today to the wedding of Jeanette and Chris.'

As soon as she said that Chris's dad pulled out his hanky and was blubbing like a baby. I looked at him and thought, 'Oh no! You're going to set me off now.' Chris still hadn't even looked at me at this point; his nerves had got the better of him. Chris's dad had normally been a man who didn't show his feelings, but as he had got older he had become a more emotional person and he cried the whole way through the ceremony.

I had asked the photographer not to take too many staged photographs; I wanted a lot of random pictures. The company I had booked was called 'Dream Capture' and I wanted them to catch the moment as it happened, and they did get one of Chris's dad crying like a baby.

When Chris did eventually have to face me he was clearly shocked and had to look twice to make sure it really was me. But then said he had never seen me look as lovely. I felt so special – like a little Cheryl Cole!

When we came to saying our vows, there were a lot of tears from me and when we arrived at the bit where we had to say 'I do', I had visions of Chris saying 'No I don't; see you later!' but of course he didn't.

During the ceremony we had a poem read out that had been written specially for these occasions. The registrar had shown me a selection of these poems and as soon as I saw this one, I couldn't believe how much it summed us up. It was all about us, how we felt so special for each other, how much we had been through together and how far we had come. It was beautifully written.

The pictures of us signing the register were hilarious with me, Chris, his dad and my stepdad Mark, who is only 4ft nothing. He was standing next to Chris as Chris signed the register, but because he was so small it appeared on the picture as if he was sitting down next to him.

We had other music played throughout including 'Here and Now' from Luther Van Dross, and we walked out to Leona Lewis's 'Footprints in the Sand'. That song meant so much to us and even today it makes me cry every time I hear it. We also had that song for our first dance that night at the reception.

Once the wedding ceremony was over we all went through to the main reception room and we had a drink, but every drink I got was taken off me or somehow mysteriously disappeared. This was because the photographers kept coming wanting more pictures and people wanted us to have our pictures taken with them. Some of these photographs were taken outside and I spent half the time huddled up in Chris's jacket because it was so cold. The rain had eased off, but it still felt cold and damp.

So every time the photographer called us I would give my drink to someone to hold for me until I got back – probably only had a sip from it, and when I went back to it, it had gone. Asked where it was I was told, 'I thought you'd given it me!' I thought, 'Great! I'm never going to get sloshed at this rate.'

By the time all the photos had been done and we had got back inside, everyone was half-cut, and all the canapés had gone, but things did settle down and we had a fantastic sit-down meal.

We had a choice of starter: Mozzarella cheese salad or soup, followed by the main course which was roast sirloin of beef with selection of freshly cooked vegetables and this was absolutely gorgeous. Then we had a choice of sweets with either Pavlova or cheesecake. And we had wines with the meal so I finally got a drink!

After the meal it came to the speeches. Chris's dad was up first and as soon as he started there were more tears. After he had thanked everyone for coming, he had read all the greetings cards and one in particular caught his attention. Someone had put £1,000 in the envelope, but it was all fake notes; there was only Chris's dad who didn't know this and said he thought he should get married again if people gave presents like that these days.

He was about to sit down when my uncle gave him an envelope, he said it was from someone who couldn't make the wedding. He asked Chris's dad if he would read it out. It was a card offering us their best wishes and was signed by, 'Mr & Mrs R. Sole'. Chris's dad was a very serious man, I don't know if he had got the joke, even though the whole room was in uproar he managed to keep a completely straight face.

Then it was my stepdad Mark's turn. The table we were on was raised above the rest of the guests and with Mark being so short he could hardly see over the top of the table. Suddenly a huge shout went up and Chris's mum, who was sat next to him shouted out, 'Go Mark!' I couldn't see a thing at that point and I only found out later that as my stepdad had stood up to make his speech his trousers had fallen down.

Our reception was great. During our dance to 'Footprints in the Sand' everybody was crying, because everybody who knew Chris and me and what we had been through knew those words meant so much to us.

I had arranged for what was called a 'Balloon Bomb' to go off above our heads as we were dancing. It was loaded with lots of smaller balloons and glitter and all sorts of other stuff. But I had forgotten it was there (probably because I'd organised so bloody much to happen that day). When it went off, it went with such a bang, just as the song reached its most magic moment; then all this glitter and stardust and balloons showered down on us as we were dancing. It was fantastic. Chris wanted to pick me up, but I wouldn't let him.

I'd also arranged for a light aircraft to fly over at a specific time pulling a banner behind it that read 'Mr & Mrs Badger, Just Married 6/6/09'. I had arranged that the pilot would ring me at the precise moment. So I had my phone stuffed down my bra ready to take the call. And when it rang and I was fiddling about down my bra, the photographer caught the scene perfectly.

I answered the call and told everyone to look up to the West side of the hotel. We all went outside and looked up. We heard the plane before we saw it, and then when it came into view everybody cheered and clapped us. Then before we went back inside we had some huge nets full of balloons and we just let the lot go off into the sky.

As the night went on, we had two bars open for our guests and had a lovely cold buffet organised as well as a chocolate fountain for the younger ones. I'd booked the DJ and had asked him to include a karaoke for the night, but he let us down with the karaoke and I had been looking forward to singing.

In the middle of all this Chris and I decided to go up to our room and get changed. My feet were killing me so I took my shoes off and we just had a brew and chilled for a bit. When we eventually came back down, the entire buffet had gone; we hadn't realised that everything was set to a time and we'd missed out. Maybe we had taken longer than we should have done and there were one or two who had suspicions as to what we had been up to, but they were wrong. We had both been so shattered that we just rested for a bit and forgot about the time.

The night was wonderful and I did end up as drunk as a skunk – it didn't help me being so tired, and everyone buying me beer all night. I couldn't remember getting to our room that night. Chris said I just collapsed on the bed when we got to our room and that was it. The next thing I knew was Chris waking me up and saying we hadn't long before we would have to leave the room.

Most of the family stayed at the hotel that night apart from those who had come on the coach, they all went back to Leyland. That morning I went down to breakfast in my pyjamas, dressing gown and slippers. Little did any of the other guests know that I had only just put them on! I'd slept in the clothes I'd been wearing all night, and we got the usual ribbing from everybody asking us if we'd had a night to remember. I told them, 'I don't remember a thing.'

After breakfast we went back to the room and got changed. We went down to the foyer and waited for our stuff to come through. We had all our clothes from the night before and presents and flowers etc.

We said all our goodbyes to those who were going back to Ireland, and they went straight back to the airport from the hotel. Chris's dad and his wife, Ina, had decided to stay over with us for a couple of weeks. When we got back and unloaded all the stuff we just put it in our bedroom and it was like a bomb-site; we couldn't move.

There was a sensitive time when we all arrived back at our house. Chris's mum and his stepmum hadn't spoken a word to each other. His mum had been very hurt at having lost the love of her life to this other woman and found it very hard to bring herself to talk to her.

We had all arrived back at our house and were having a cup of tea. The men could feel the tension and had decided to take their tea out in the garden. But there was no need to worry. Chris's mum broke the silence by asking Ina which was her tea on the table, and from there on they seemed reasonably fine. There wasn't the feeling they would ever be best friends, but at least they were talking.

Later that afternoon Chris's mum, her niece Sarah and his aunt and uncle went back to Ireland, but before they went, they all said what a wonderful time they'd had and apart from that it had eased the tension between Chris's mum and stepmum and since then they have got on really well. They met again at a christening over in Ireland. Chris's mum told me some time later that she had begun to realise that in fairness, Ina had been with Thomas for longer than she had and she accepted it now.

In one way I felt that because I'd done all the organising, and because I had tried to cram so much into the day, I couldn't really relax and enjoy it as I should have done. But we had had the most wonderful time. It was a wedding to remember. I have only ever seen weddings like ours in *OK* magazine, it was that good! The only difference was, there was no magazine paying us a million pounds for our wedding photoshoot.

16

IVF and pregnancy

In the months that followed our wedding, everything was looking good. We had finished the work on the house, the business was doing extremely well; in fact I had just come up with an idea for the schools that I was really excited about. But above all that, both Chris and myself were feeling so much better in ourselves healthwise.

I don't think I had felt so good for years; everything was the best it had been in all the time we had been together and it got me thinking that maybe I would like another baby. I sat Chris down one night in August that year and told him how I was feeling; he said he thought I had been planning something like this, because a couple of years before we had said that if we had any more children we would need a bigger house and a bigger car. Then he started to say things like, 'Do you remember a while back we talked about this saying if we have another child, we'll need a bigger house and a bigger car, and what about having a business to run as well? Now we have a five-bedroom house and seven-seater car … You've been planning this.'

He didn't rule it out; he was just outlining how he thought it might affect our lives. But Chris knew me by now and he knew that once I'd made up my mind about something, I wouldn't give in.

I went to see my doctor and explained how I was feeling and told her that I wanted to try for another baby. The main concern was of course my health and how it had been in the past, but I assured her that I had never felt better and told her that I was sure I would be fine. Then she raised the matter that a couple of years earlier, I'd had my tubes tied and she said, because I already had children, she didn't think the NHS would be willing to untie them because they said I would probably want them tying again at some later stage.

She said the only possible option was if I was to have IVF. But she said there was no way the NHS would pay for me to have IVF and that if I wanted it I would have to go private.

'Right, put me in for it then', I told her.

So my doctor got the ball rolling and by October 2009 I had an appointment to see a specialist at a clinic called 'Care' in Manchester. It wasn't very far from St Mary's hospital where I'd attended for my bowel problems. I was still having problems with my bowel, it was by now manageable but by no means as it should have been.

So I went along to see the specialist and after he had looked at my notes he explained that due to the type of procedure I'd had when my tubes had been tied it was highly unlikely they would be able to reverse it. He said the best option for me was IVF. But he was concerned about my health, especially my heart condition, my bowel and other issues that had affected me over the years.

He said he was also worried about the number of sections I'd already had, saying the pressure of having a possible multiple birth could cause my womb to rupture. He discussed a whole range of risks involved. But he said it would be possible for me to have IVF if it was what I really wanted. I said it was and explained that I was feeling better than I had ever done for years.

He asked when my last period had been and I asked him if we could start it right away. The doctor said no, I would have to wait another month. He said the drugs would be sent to me by courier. The drugs had to be injected by me, some into my stomach and some into my leg. I have always been terrified of needles and I knew there was no way I could do this so Chris agreed to do it for me. The injections would have to be administered at the exact same time every day and this had to be strictly kept to.

A couple of days later a letter arrived from the clinic, which had been copied to my doctor. It suggested I only have one egg implanted due to the risks involved. This was because of my heart problems and the fact that if I were to have two babies it would mean there would be two more heartbeats going on inside me and this could cause problems. He did say I could have two, but recommended only having the one. Me being me, I said I would have what I wanted! The first stage was to begin the drug treatment.

A few days later the drugs arrived and we started on the day we were told to and Chris gave me the first injection at the prescribed time. Chris had to make sure he was home in time to give me the injection. And all went well until one day when Chris hadn't got home and time was running out fast. I was panicking because I knew if he wasn't there, I would have to do it myself.

It got closer and closer to the time and I had been getting so desperate, because I knew it had to be done at that set time otherwise the whole cycle was void. I had the needle at the ready. I counted ... 'One... two ... three' and stuck it in my leg, but before I could press the syringe and inject the drug into my leg; I panicked again and pulled the needle straight out again. This went on for ages. My leg was like a dartboard – I had done it ten times before I finally got it right! My leg was so bruised after that. When Chris came home that morning I went so mad at him, he was never late again!

This process went on for a month during that time; the drugs were to increase the amount of eggs my ovaries produced. I had to keep going back to the clinic for regular scans so they could see how the eggs in my ovaries were developing and how many there were there and when they had developed properly they could be removed.

I could see all this going on in the scan, but I kept being told they weren't ready yet, so I would go back again a few days later. The eggs on the scan looked huge – like oranges, but of course they were only very tiny.

On 5th December the day came for me to go to the clinic to have my eggs expelled. Chris had already had to have his sperm tested to see if it was healthy and up to this point, that hadn't been a problem because I had been able to help him with producing the sample. But on this day in December he had to do it all by himself.

Everything is done in sequence. I was sent down to the theatre and put under anaesthetic because they had to push a big needle into my ovaries and suck out the bubbles – hoping there would be eggs in the bubbles they removed.

While all this is going on Chris had to go to another room and produce his sperm. The way he explained it to me was hilarious; he said he was sent into a room and told to produce, but nothing would work. To make it worse there was a nurse right outside the door waiting to take it off him.

So there he was in this cold blank room with nothing more than some girly magazines and an impatient nurse at the other side of a door. With nothing working he was worried that there wouldn't be anything there for when I had come out of theatre. He said the pressure was really on. It took him ages and when he handed the sample to her, he said she looked at it and then looked at him as if to say, 'Is that it?'

When I got back to the recovery room and I came round, Chris was there with his head down to the ground as if someone had died. I was about to ask him what the matter was when the doctor came in, still in his blue gown and hat.

'Right, I am pleased to tell you both that we have got four eggs and they are being fertilized at the moment, and I am pleased to tell you, Chris, that your sperm are absolutely fine.' Chris's face lit up.

On the way home afterwards although I was in quite a lot of pain, I couldn't stop laughing at Chris telling me how he had struggled that morning. I was almost wetting myself.

The following day we sat waiting for the phone to ring. The doctor had said that he had hoped a young girl like me might produce as many as fourteen eggs, but they only had four and the main concern they had was, under normal circumstances if we start with say six eggs, you may only end up with two, because they don't all take and develop. My disappointment was, I had started with four and I was worried that I could end up with none. The phone rang and the doctor told us it was good news.

'Two eggs have fertilized and two haven't, we will keep our eye on them and let you know in a couple of days how they are doing.' It was as if they were babysitting. It was really weird.

Although the doctor had said that was good news, I wasn't convinced. I was thinking it was failure! Only two eggs, and they might not grow; I could easily lose them both.

Two days later the phone rang ...

'Good news, we still have two eggs and they have both grown well. One of them is a grade A, and the other is grade B. They are both good. Give it another day and we will get you booked in to have them implanted.'

It is only on the day that you're going to have them put in that you actually get to make your mind up how many you're going to have. I remember getting up on the morning and wondering what the hell to expect.

We got there and we were sent to a different waiting room. I was really nervous and I kept going to the tea machine every ten minutes. If I can't have a cigarette I have to have tea, I'm terrible like that. I had seen these other couples who had gone in before us and as they were coming out they looked happy, but at the same time they seemed scared.

Then a thought came into my head that they hadn't been in there that long. My mind kept telling me, God! If I wasn't in long, the eggs might slide out and I'd lose them. They were only the size of a pin-prick!

Eventually we were called in and we got gowned up and ready. It is probably one of the most undignified processes ever. I was laid flat on my back with my legs raised and in some kind of stirrups and wide apart. The doctor came in and told us, 'Do you know Jeanette, the egg that was a grade B has changed to a grade A overnight. What do you want to do, how many do you want us to put in?'

I told him I wanted them both in: there was no way I was leaving one on its own and I couldn't choose between them.

Before they started they came in with a picture of the eggs in a dish. They had been magnified because they were so small. Then they brought the eggs in and the whole procedure was like a military process, because they don't want to drop them.

First they place a long tube that is on the end of a syringe into the dish and suck up the eggs. Then they check the dish to make sure the eggs are not still there. They then implanted the eggs inside me using the tube which I couldn't help thinking looked like a turkey baster.

After they had done that, they take the tube away and rinse it into another dish to make sure the eggs had gone where they should have done. After the doctor checked, he said, 'There we are, two babies in there; just stay on the bed for a couple of minutes and then you can get up.'

I said 'Are you sure? Will they not fall out?' and they all burst out laughing, but the doctor assured me they wouldn't. He told me that there was a muscle in there that would hold everything in place.

During the process the doctor, who was an Indian man, had played some weird Indian music. I felt like I was in a mosque, but it was his choice of music and in one way it was quite relaxing. After a few minutes I got up and got dressed. The staff gave us a pregnancy testing kit, but told us not to test before 24th December. It was one of those that I had to do and then send back to them to be tested.

We were going over to Chris's parents during the holidays, around 16th December to hand over the Christmas presents. Before I went I had decided that I wanted to know for sure if I was pregnant so I went to the chemists and got one of the best kits you can get. This one tells you if you're pregnant even before you've missed your period.

I did the test and it came back negative. I was gutted! We went over to Ireland to Chris's parents for a break believing that we'd been through it all for nothing. We spent the next week or so worrying. I had been told not to do the test before the 24th and that was the day we were due to come back home.

On the morning of Christmas Eve, we were ready to come back home from Ireland. I'd left everything organised at home, my mum was collecting our turkey and everything else for us. I'd already sorted all the presents out before we'd left.

I got up that morning and went to the bathroom; I'd left Chris in bed. I thought, 'Shall I do another test?' I had a test kit left over and I'd brought it with me. I did the test and looked at it. Then I checked the box again to see if I'd read the result properly. I ran into the bedroom and woke Chris – 'Chris, Chris, I'm pregnant!' I said to him.

'No you're not, don't be daft', he replied.

I said 'I am … look!'

He looked at the test and said, 'I bloody well told you not to do it early; they told you, not before the 24th, but you never listen do you?'

When we got home that afternoon I rang Manchester and told them I'd done the test and asked them if it meant I really was pregnant.

'Oh yes, if it says you are, then you are!' She told me that you can never get a wrong result: if it says positive, it is positive. It is all due to the hormone that reacts to the test and it can't lie. I kept that pregnancy test in my bag for weeks after to show everyone I met that I was pregnant.

On 27th December we went back to Manchester to the clinic to have an eight-week scan to confirm. The nurse asked us if we wanted to know how many babies there were. We said we did, but my thoughts were there must be loads because we knew that each egg could divide and produce more babies.

'You have the two original eggs you started with', she said. 'Both the eggs that were implanted have taken as single babies, and are looking just fine.'

She showed us a picture and even though they weren't fully formed you just knew they were two little people, they were so cute!

After that eight-week scan in Manchester we were discharged into the community, so my next job was to make an appointment with our own local midwife and I did. But everyone I saw kept saying how they couldn't believe they had allowed me to become pregnant with all the health issues I had, but I told them I felt really well.

Things were very different by the time I was five months into the pregnancy. I was feeling pretty rough and certainly didn't feel fit enough at all; I was feeling really bad. But I knew I had to keep on going because it was what I wanted, but it got very, very tough. I had to learn to accept that it was going to be tough and just get on with it.

From then on all my care throughout the rest of my pregnancy could only be provided by a senior consultant due to the fact that I was such a complicated case and that made it very awkward. Whenever I went to see the midwife, if I had any questions she couldn't help me because all decisions were down to the consultant and nobody else could do or say anything without his say so.

The main concern the consultant had, was my bowel. Because I had trouble emptying my bowel, she was worried that I would become too compacted and the weight of the twins would make things worse, and that they could become restricted too because of that. She also had concerns that the drugs (laxatives) that I had been on to expel my bowel could make me go into premature labour.

As the pregnancy advanced, the demand on my heart was greater and this was another concern. On top of all that I still had my business to run and a family to look after. I was told I needed to slow down. I was in absolute agony, but I couldn't slow down; I had far too much to do.

We were both keen to know the sex of our babies as well. We already had three girls and with there being two babies in there, there was a good chance that one of them was a boy. I booked in to have all sorts of scans done. At sixteen weeks I ended up paying out to have 4D Babybond scans. This is a really in-depth scan that shows everything. I was there waiting at their door and looking at the images for little winkly bits, but nothing! I did the same at twenty weeks and was told they were definitely two girls.

The Babybond scan can be taken as a video and it is absolutely amazing, you can see them so vividly and watch all their movements and facial expressions. We could see them opening their eyes and sucking their thumbs. Then one of them would push the other out of the way as if they wanted to get nearer to the camera.

That was the fun side of being pregnant, but on the whole it was a real struggle. I had a lot of pressure pain and couldn't sleep for it. The doctor thought it may be coming from old scar tissue and he was worried that it could rupture, and although it was painful and I did have to slow down to some extent, I had to keep going as best I could.

There was one particular day when I had gone up to a nursery to cover for a member of staff who had gone off sick. I got there and being in pain and not thinking straight, I parked the car and it was on a bit of a hill, but I hadn't put the handbrake on properly and the car started to roll backwards. Not thinking, I ran after the car and tried to get in to stop it. I should have just let it go, but I did manage to stop it after yanking the handbrake on.

I had hurt myself. I did the job and I got by – I had cleaned the nursery, but when Chris found out he went ballistic at me. I had a scan to make sure everything was all right and luckily it was. I started to realise afterwards that I should be taking it easier at that stage, and I did. I did travel out to some of the jobs, but I didn't do any cleaning.

There was another incident when I was at home. I had been doing some washing and was about to fold up a tablecloth that I'd washed. I hadn't noticed, but it had fallen onto the wooden floor and I'd stood on it. Because it was a silky material I slipped and went flying onto my back. That was another trip up to the hospital.

I also once fell down the stairs. I had so many lucky escapes, and Chris was in tears sometimes because he was sure I was going to lose the babies; he wanted them so much and was so worried. I was also having checks for my own problems. It felt like I was never away from the doctors or the hospital. I was now beginning to feel like I was under a lot of stress at that time.

At 28 weeks I wanted them out of me; I'd had enough. I had gone to see my consultant a few times and had said to her how I felt, but she kept saying to me, 'I need to get you further, it would be too dangerous to consider it yet. I will get you to 34 weeks and definitely deliver them then.'

I pestered her again a few weeks later and she got her diary out and said, 'Right, let's have a look. I will deliver them on July 16th, that will take you to 34 weeks.' So I agreed to that and went along with her decision. She did say that it could of course happen naturally before that date. After that morning it did reassure me and at least I had something to focus on.

When the day to go in finally arrived I hadn't slept the whole night before, due to nerves and because I was in pain. I had been at the hospital the day before. I had gone because I thought I was going into labour. The doctors and nurses had examined me and although my cervix was dilated by about one centimetre I wasn't having any contractions so they sent me home. They were determined I was going to go to the agreed date.

When we got to the hospital we were on the neonatal unit just in case there were any problems with the babies. They'd also had a machine brought in to recirculate my blood in case there was a problem and I lost a lot of blood. There was also a heart specialist on standby because of my heart problems.

My dad also made an appearance. My brother Milton had told him what was happening and warned him of the complications.

'Hiya Net,' he put his arm around me and shook Chris's hand like nothing had ever happened. 'I just thought I'd be here today', he said.

That was the first time I'd seen him since we'd had words. Here he was at the hospital with us and he wasn't very chatty. Chris was a bit bemused and a little annoyed by him just turning up after what had happened. I was too, but when I was lying on that trolley I suddenly noticed his nose and remembered how he had looked years before.

I hadn't been there long when the nurses came in and told us we were going down and I was glad about that, I hate hanging around in those places; I would much rather be getting on with it. When we got downstairs Chris was sent to get gowned-up and I was taken into theatre. I was getting very nervous by this time. My consultant came in to see me, 'Well here we are Jeanette, at last, let's get it done', and she went off to get herself scrubbed up and ready. By the time she was ready we should have been ready to start. I was going to have an epidural for the procedure, but they were having lots of problems getting the anaesthetic into my spine.

I didn't know this and I said to the woman who was doing the anaesthetics, 'You're really good at this.'

Normally when I have had them before they have been pretty painful, especially the first injection they give to numb you before they put the thing in, but I couldn't feel a thing this time. Time was going on and they were getting really confused, moving it about here and there then all of a sudden she shouted, 'Oh God, Oh God, it's come out too fast!' They had to put a stopper on the end of the tube. Then they had to test the fluid, which I later found out was spinal fluid and resituate the injection all over again. It took them nearly an hour before they could finally start properly and all this time they were comforting me and saying how well I was doing, but I couldn't feel a thing.

The doctor was asking me if I could feel any sensation down my legs, but I couldn't. I told her I could feel a strange feeling across my belly. She was moving it about, then I felt a really weird sensation go down one leg, and then I felt a massive pressure on my other leg and the same sensation go down that. I told them I could feel that and they said 'Brilliant!' Then they suddenly whipped me around on this bed.

I told them I could still feel my legs and I was bending them and saying, 'Look I can bend them, I'm not having you on', and I demonstrated. I was told not to worry, that it would soon take effect. From there on it became such a quick procedure after that. By this time I was feeling a little anxious and headachy. An hour had passed and I could still feel what was happening. Normally my legs would have felt like lead by now, but they didn't.

I kept telling them I could feel my feet and started to wiggle my feet for them, but I was told everything was OK and not to worry. As soon as they began to cut me open to start the delivery, I could feel what they were doing.

'I can feel it, I can feel it!' I said.

The doctor looked at me and said, 'OK, what am I doing?'

'You're nipping me', I said. Then the doctor gave me another injection of something that was much better. The doctor warned me not to worry if the babies didn't cry straight away when they were born; she said this would be normal with a birth of this kind.

'OK, that's one baby out!' They took her away and we didn't hear any crying. They struggled a bit to get the other baby out; it was as if she was saying 'No, I'm not leaving here, it's nice and warm in here', but eventually she was born and we waited for a while before finally heard them cry; first one and then the other.

Chris and me were in floods of tears when we heard them. The nurses asked why we were crying. We told them it was because we were so happy.

17

Two beautiful baby girls

The consultant told us the babies were both very healthy and that they could come straight to the ward with me. I thought, so much for me getting some sleep. I had been hoping to have a few days' rest.

Chris was passed the babies and he went outside to the waiting area while they stitched me and checked me out for any damage to my other scar tissue. When they wheeled me out after about twenty minutes, Chris was waiting there in the corridor with one on each arm, but he was concerned and said to the nurse, 'I think there is something wrong, they've been making funny noises and I didn't know what to do.' He hadn't said anything to anyone because he knew they were busy sorting me out in theatre. The nurse had a look at them and whisked them off to the neonatal ward. Alicia was making grunting noises, but was coping just about. But Fiona had stopped breathing altogether and they had to work on her to bring her round.

We weren't allowed to see them and this was upsetting. As all this was happening the anaesthetist came out and saw me. She looked at me and said, 'Jeanette I'm not happy with you, you're a funny colour and your eye is all droopy.'

I knew it was, but I thought that was probably due to

lack of sleep and they were trying to shut themselves.

I was taken to the delivery ward for the first night for them to keep an eye on me. I didn't sleep all that night, even though I was as tired as I was. I had a terrible head-ache and I was just hungry the whole time. The nurses just kept checking me and bringing me food. I don't know what it was, but I was absolutely starving.

The next morning they took me down to the wards to give me a bath and make me more comfortable. The nurse said they would let me go and see the twins once I had been sorted out, but I asked them if we could go on the way down so they agreed they would do that.

When I saw Fiona all wired up and on the ventilator, it was so upsetting. Alicia seemed to be doing well, but they had kept her there just as a precaution. The strange thing was I found myself attaching myself more to Alicia at that point. I think that was because I was scared of allowing myself to get too close to Fiona for fear she wasn't going to make it.

Once down on the maternity ward the nurses there were so overrun, so busy. There was one poor woman who was screaming like mad in pain and she kept us all awake all night that first night on that ward, then they took her back down to theatre the following morning and found she had ruptured her bladder after having a caesarean. We had all been calling her all the names under the sun for keeping us awake, the poor girl!

I found it really tough on the ward because all the other new mums had their babies with them, and my hormones were all over the place, and I was on a ward where all the babies would be waking all night, and instinctively as soon as I heard them cry, I woke up too. I was going mental. One of my legs still wasn't right at this stage and one was, but I didn't know why and I was in agony.

There was one time when the nurse had given me a blood-thinning injection and then not long after came to give me another. I told her she had just given me that injection, but she was adamant she hadn't. I argued with her that she had and when she checked she apologised and said it was because she was so busy; she hadn't written it up in my notes. That really scared me because that injection could have killed me. I became very untrusting of them at that point.

I even took myself to the shower in a wheelchair. I put my bad leg on the chair and pushed myself along using my good leg. The sweat was pouring out of me, but it was the only way I could have a shower and I knew I needed one, I stank!

It got so bad that I was crying all the time. I needed painkillers for my headache and I would ask the nurse for them, but they would forget and it could be ages before I got them. The only time I was happy was when Chris came. I would get him to take me up to see the babies and leave me there.

I got more sympathy and help from the staff up there than I did from those on the ward and when they found out that I was on a ward with new mothers and their babies, they spoke to the sister and suggested that I should be on the pre-natal ward. So the next day I was hoping this was going to happen, and it did, but I hadn't been there long before they began to fill that ward too with mothers and new babies.

I was told that after three days I might be able to go home. My leg had started to work apart from the odd blip when it would give way. The doctor said I would have to go downstairs to have a postnatal examination and if all was well I could go home. I went down and they found that my legs were swollen and I was still having headaches, but I'd put this down to lack of sleep.

They sent for a senior doctor to come and see me, and she listened to my chest and could hear that something wasn't right. She wrote down all manner of things connected to what my heart was doing. She rang a heart specialist and explained my case. The heart specialist suggested an abdominal scan and a heart scan. I was sent for the scans. I walked there with swollen legs and stitches in my belly and it was quite a long way from the ward.

When I got there, I was seen by a gorilla of a doctor who spoke very little and only when he had to. 'Get on the bed.'

'Yes sir!' I felt like it was a command and I should have saluted him.

The report said something about a problem with my internal and external intra-vena cava being enlarged to 30 millimetres, and heart failure.

'What now?' I asked him.

'You can go back to your ward', I was told. So off I went and I walked all the way back again.

I was allowed home later that day on the condition that I came back every day to the postnatal unit. I arranged it that I would go down there at the same time I was visiting the twins. I called in the following day which was Saturday, and I saw the nurse who said she would bleep the doctor who would be down as soon as he could. I said I was going up to see the twins but the nurse wasn't happy about me going.

'I really don't think you should go up there Jeanette, this is quite scary; I think you'd be better off waiting here until you have seen the doctor', she said.

I explained that I'd been at home all night and asked her to call me as soon as someone was there to see me. I waited there all day, but no one came. No one bothered!

Monday came and I went back again. They were full of apologies for what had happened on the Saturday. The nurse bleeped the doctor again, but again I waited all day and no one came.

On the Tuesday I was visiting the twins and found out that I'd had a phone call to go down and see the doctor, but it was too late, I'd missed him. The message had been left with neonatal and hadn't been given to me until it was too late.

I went in again on the Wednesday to see the twins and was told the doctor wanted to see me – at last!

'I think we could do with you staying in hospital, you are in danger of suffering heart failure', they said.

I argued back saying, 'What? After all this time, you've known about this, but nobody could be bothered to come down to see me before this; well I'm not staying in hospital, my swellings are going down now anyway.'

He brought up the matter of my scan and the fact that my heart had been slightly enlarged, but where the veins attach to my heart was fine, it was just a little swollen further down. I never got to find out why they were like that. And as time went on we got on with things and the twins came home in the August.

Around the time the twins had been born I had received compensation for criminal injuries overseas, for rape and psychological injury, which the army had helped with. I got a letter one day telling me to sign if I was prepared to accept what they were offering. I signed and sent it straight back. I had the cheque within a week, which was great with just having twins to look after.

Straight away I had seen this very expensive pram that I liked and wanted for them both. The business was doing well, but you can't very well buy a pram and book it to the business. It was called a 'High Candy Peach' and it was just the size of a normal push-chair, but it was so light and had everything possible except for an engine. It cost me £2,000, but it was amazing. Even when they had grown out of it and I sold it, I still got £900 for it.

It was a hard time for me because I just wouldn't rest or take a back seat. I was looking after the twins and running the business too, and in between all this I was trying to breastfeed the twins and was expressing breast milk for feeds during the night.

The problem was that because of the stress I was under I was getting less and less milk, and the less I got, the more desperate I was becoming and the more I tried to express the milk the sorer I became. Before the twins came home I had to provide milk for them in hospital and I was struggling. I could see all these bottles in the fridge from other mums and I'd have just one bottle. There was only once that I managed to get loads and I got quite excited about it, but it didn't happen again and I was back to square one and upset about it.

Because I was feeding two babies the hospital gave me two pumping machines and I felt like a cow in a milking parlour, and one day when I was in the bedroom expressing the milk Emma walked in and saw what I was doing. I had the two machines going on full power. She fell about laughing, 'What are you doing?' she asked. I explained the best I could because by now, I was also laughing my head off at the look on her face.

'Is that what cows do?' she asked. I just laughed more and couldn't answer her. It is the way Emma is, bless her; she says it just as she sees it.

I was really struggling to get the milk so much so that I was becoming very weepy. I told the nurses at the neonatal unit and they suggested I take some of the babies' clothes and smell them. They thought it might help me to relax and feel closer to them, and by doing that I might get more milk, but it didn't really work and in the end I had to give up.

18

Brain surgery

By August we had the twins home and life was easier in some respects, but it was also hard as well, having a family of five children now instead of just three. I was still having problems with headaches, and one day I had gone to see my doctor. My vision was jumping up and down, I thought because I hadn't really rested, I'd been getting up and down night and day to see to the babies and I'd been so busy, it was unreal.

There had also been a serious problem with work and this had created a lot of tension between me and Chris. It had got to the point where we were hardly speaking. This extremely bad patch lasted for a good while and I learnt afterwards that Chris had even suggested to his mum that he might move back home to Ireland. This situation didn't help with the problems I was having with my health, although they were certainly not the cause of those problems.

When my doctor saw me she immediately took some blood tests. She could see that I was severely anaemic. I was very pale and also my heart rate was quite fast, but the main concern for me was the headaches. The doctor gave me a prescription for some iron pills to take and told me to get them right away. She said she would probably be giving me a ring later that night. She suspected I would have to go into hospital for a blood transfusion.

That night I waited by the phone for it to ring, expecting to have to go in for the transfusion, but it never came. There was no phone call and no message from my doctor either so I assumed everything must have been all right and that they had expected the iron tablets would put right whatever was wrong.

By September we were getting back to normal and we were beginning to get over what had caused us to fall out. One Sunday morning we were feeling more loved up than we had done since well before the twins had been born and for the first time in ages we made love. It wasn't furiously mad sex or anything like that.

But I screamed out in agony. My neck and my arms had become paralysed and I had a massive pain to my head. I couldn't move or feel anything in my upper body. Chris rang for an ambulance right away and I was taken to casualty at Chorley Hospital. By the time I got there and was seen by the doctor, I was beginning to get a bit of feeling back. I had to explain everything to the doctor and his conclusion was that I had probably pulled a muscle.

He told me to see how I went on and if the pain was still there after a couple of days, to go back. It was still there; I was in agony. I rang my dad and he said he would run me down to the hospital. Chris stayed with the twins. When I got there it was the same doctor who had seen me on the Sunday morning.

He said he would run some more tests and send me for an MRI scan, so off I went and they sorted me out and sent me into the scanner. After a short while, they pulled me out and said they wanted to scan my brain.

'Why do you want to do that, are you saying I've lost it that much that I need my head testing or something?' I asked them.

But they assured me that they just wanted to have a look. They put a frame around my neck and head and sent me into the scanner again. After about fifteen minutes of being in there I was told to wait outside and the doctor would see me in due course.

He called me in and said I had a slipped disc in my neck and that he had also found a problem at the base of my brain. He assured me it was all right and that it might just be a congenital condition and might not cause me any problems, but he said he was going to refer me to Neurology to sort out my slipped disc because it was impinging on my nerve and my spinal cord slightly.

He showed me on the scan what the problem was but hadn't said outright what it was. The best way I can describe it was that it looked like a small cauliflower that had dropped down at the base of my brain. Now I'm terrible with anything like that. Straight away as soon as I came home I was on the computer and on the internet.

I just typed into Google something like 'cauliflower shaped thing in your head' and it came up. Obviously other people had discussed this and had described it that way. There it was: Cerebellum. I investigated more and went on to look at some pictures and it called it Arnold Chiari Malformation Type 1.

I began to look at causes and it described how childbirth and the possible loss of spinal fluid could be the reason. The type that I had of this condition was the only type that could be acquired. There were other types, but they were all conditions that you were born with, so I immediately associated mine with what had happened in the hospital when I was giving birth to the twins. I had lost spinal fluid that day during the course of having my epidural.

I had been told at the hospital to go to my GPs the following morning, which was the Wednesday, to get a referral to see a neurologist; so I went along and told him what had happened. He said he would have to find out from the hospital exactly what they had found. I explained the best I could about seeing something that resembled a cauliflower at the base of my brain.

It took until 5th October for my notes to come through from the hospital. I asked my GP how long it would be before I was seen by the neurologist. He said he was hoping it would only be a couple of weeks; he was going to put it to the surgeon. I asked if there was a number I could ring for anybody who deals with appointments, and he said there was. He gave me a number that was like a triage centre where all referrals from all GPs are sent to first, and from there they arrange your appointment.

I rang them and they confirmed that I was on the list, but they told me there was a twelve-week waiting list, so I said OK and I accepted that. I waited patiently for about eight weeks and then I rang them again. I figured that by this time they would have a date for my slot. I asked them if they had me down for an appointment because I was now eight weeks in from my referral.

'I'm sorry, Mrs Badger, we haven't got you down on the system.'

I said, 'What do you mean I haven't got an appointment?'

She told me that she would look into it and ring me back. She did ring back and I was told the neurologist had looked at my case and referred me to see the surgeon, but there was a twelve-week waiting list for that.

'Hold on, why has he referred me to the surgeon?' I knew that you were only sent to the surgeon if you needed surgery and apart from that, I had already waited for eight weeks and now I was being told that I will have to wait another twelve weeks. I was fuming. I rang my own doctors' surgery and spoke to the secretary.

I explained what had happened and asked if there was anyone I could see privately. I said I had already waited eight weeks and didn't want to have to wait another twelve weeks. I wasn't getting any better. I had trouble picking the babies up, I was very weak in my upper limbs and I was in constant pain, especially in my head.

The only good thing as far as my health was concerned was that my bowel had seemed to miraculously heal itself. I'd had to come off the laxatives while I was pregnant and I found that my bowel was functioning – not completely normally, but if I reminded myself that I should go, I did and it worked. That was one thing the doctors were over the moon about.

She explained how the mix-up had come about with the referrals and agreed with me that it was a ridiculous situation. She immediately got me a number for a consultant at Moor Park in Preston; a neurosurgeon. I rang and made an appointment to see the surgeon a couple of days later.

I said to Chris to go into work, I would be all right going on my own and that he should look after the work side of things, because we couldn't just drop everything. Straight away my dad said, 'Well I'm coming, you're not going on your own; I want to hear what they have to say.'

So me and my dad went off to Moor Park to see the surgeon. We had a good talk, I told him about all the problems I'd been having. He looked at my notes and straight away he said I definitely needed surgery. He warned me that I was in serious danger of becoming paralysed, because it had already happened once, and I was very lucky that I'd got my feeling and mobility back. He said it could very easily happen again and next time I might not be as lucky.

He suggested it should be done soon and if possible within the next six weeks. He said he would refer me back to the surgeon at the hospital, but by now I had lost all confidence in the NHS and I said to him, 'No, I want you to book me in as a private patient.' He took his glasses off and almost choked.

'What, private?' he asked me again. I told him that was what I wanted. He worked in the NHS as well as doing private, but I could tell that he was good and from the way he had spoken to me and explained things I knew there and then that I wanted him to take me on as his patient. His name was Dr Gurusinghe, a lovely Indian man. Although he covered all brain surgery, he specialised in Chiari Malformation Type 1. He told me that it was very dangerous surgery and explained that on a scale of 1 to 10 with 10 being the most risky, mine was about a 7 to 7.5.

He went through everything that would happen and said the most risky part of the procedure was when they had to cut into my brain, because there were some main arteries that were inside and hidden. The danger came if they cut into my brain and those arteries had moved from where they should be, I was in danger of suffering quadriplegia or a stroke.

I came away from there scared to death, fully aware of all the dangers, both if I had the surgery and if I didn't. But to me it had to be done and I left Moor Park full of confidence in Dr Gurusinghe.

I came home and spent days looking at the internet and reading of the experiences of other people who had been through this. I was searching for pictures of people to see how their heads looked after they'd had it done, all sorts of stupid things like that.

I know it is a silly thing to do, but I found comfort in doing it. I was very scared. I knew I could die if it went wrong. I knew there was a real danger of that occurring and I had Chris and my five beautiful children to consider. Chris was getting better from his PTSD and I was genuinely scared that this could tip him back over the edge and who would be there to help him and look after our children?

Every evening we would sit down and try to talk about things and every evening we would break down in tears. Chris would apologise and cry, saying he was sorry for treating me the way he had throughout the summer because of the trouble we'd had concerning that horrible work issue. But we began to realise that things like that don't matter.

All that mattered was what was happening now. The past had gone and we had to deal with the problems in front of us. I was worried because of the risks we were facing, and I could see the fear in Chris's face, but I could also see the love as well, and that gave me strength.

We had sat there for hours discussing things like my funeral arrangements and the music I wanted. There was only about two weeks to go now before my surgery and I realised that the more I got upset and worried about what might happen, the worse this was making Chris.

The last thing any of us needed was for Chris to start to go downhill and slip back to where he'd been a couple of years ago. He had been doing so well and until now it was beginning to look as if he had found a way of managing his PTSD, but my problems were now in danger of undoing all that good. I was worried, but for Chris's sake and the kids I had to be strong and come to terms with what might happen. Then I thought, 'You know what Jeanette; stop getting yourself upset, if it happens, it happens.' I said to myself that all my life had been pretty crap until I met Chris. I realised that if it was God's intention to take me now after all that had happened in my earlier years, then so be it. I had to accept it. I had had a life of two halves, and I had so much to be thankful for, for having had happiness with Chris in the second half of my life.

Once I came to terms with what might happen, I knew I had to prepare for the worst and make sure that everything was in order for those left behind, should I die. I got my solicitor to come out to the house to write my will. I had countless meetings with Tina, my secretary, who I swore to secrecy.

I made sure everything was in order for the business. I left step by step instructions on how to pay wages in, how the wages were set up, all the bank account numbers and codes, where my life insurance policies were kept and stuff like that, and all done methodically and set out simply for

Chris and Tina to follow. Poor Tina, God love her, she went through hell with me in those few weeks.

I also secretly began to write letters to all my family. One by one, I spent hours putting these letters together for each and every one of them. Chris was my biggest worry. I was so scared for him. If I did die, how would he cope? He was still very vulnerable and I was worried he would drift into depression and who would look after our five children then?

I had always said that no matter what, I would never have left him. I had always promised him that and yet here I was and the reality was that I might have to leave him. I may not have a choice in it. I wanted him to know how proud I was of him to have come this far. I wanted to get across to him that I didn't want him to let any of this get him down. I told him to promise me that he would not kill himself, to be strong; I told him that the kids would need him to be strong and that they would fill him with happiness.

I went on to try to assure him that the memory of me would live on through our children. I said that I wanted him to move on in life and if he wanted, to find someone else. I promised him I would not be offended if he did this, because he deserved to be happy.

I did however put into my letter to him that, when it was his turn, I wanted us both to be buried in the same grave. I wanted him to make this right with whoever his new partner was. There was no way I wanted to be on my own forever with all the creepy crawlies, and as long as he came to me in the end I would be happy.

Just before the surgery I told Chris that if it did go wrong, I would be watching over him in spirit. He said, 'Oh right, do me a favour then, will you be able to do the ironing and run the Hoover over the place from time to time?'

I told him not to be so cheeky, he could do that himself.

When I had done the letters, I sealed them in envelopes and gave them to Tina with strict instructions that nobody should see them unless I died. I was planning everything and leaving nothing to chance, right down to the music I wanted playing at my funeral.

Music was a big part of my life; I often related events that had happened to certain songs and to people too. It was the same for Chris; he had a similar love of music to me. I chose some songs to be played at my funeral and they were all songs that meant something to me and Chris. I wanted him to know through the songs that I was still there with him. It was a bloody hard time.

I had started to put together little keepsake boxes for the twins with small things inside that would remind them of me. I knew they were far too young to remember me, but I wanted them to know that I loved them and what sort of person their mummy had been. Chris said, 'You will never need to worry about that, I will have so much of your stuff around and photographs; this house will be like a shrine to you.' He said it jokingly, but I knew deep down, he meant it.

It was a terrible time and I know that what I did was important to me. If I hadn't done things the way I had and I had died, I felt I would have regretted it. I wanted to leave everything right especially for Chris; I knew he would have it hard enough without having to start organising everything. I had always tried to protect him from everything – all the business side and other stuff like that, and for him now to have to take charge and do all this organising would be such a struggle, I knew.

We sat in the house one day talking, and Chris asked me if there was anything in life I had ever wanted to do.

'I have always wanted to write a book and tell the world about my life, but it's too bloody late now, but I tell you, if I come round from this, I will write my book', I said to him.

'Jeanette, you will come round from this. You have far too much to give and I need you, he's not going to take someone who's needed as much as you … We all need you.' We were both getting upset and crying by now.

I said, 'Let's not talk about all that now, everything will be OK; let's just focus on the operation.'

Every night when I was in bed, I would be reading off in my head what I was going to say to my kids in the letters I was writing to them, and tears would be streaming down my face as the thoughts came into my head telling them how much I loved them, and I would have to say to them that I didn't want to leave them, but now and again things happen that we have no control over.

We had just found out that Hayley was pregnant. Things hadn't been easy all the time with Hayley. She was a teenager and like with all teenagers and their mums there were arguments, but I wanted to explain to Hayley that I loved her and was so proud of her. I knew she would make a wonderful mum.

And then there was my mum. I loved her so much, but because of our family history we had always been a little distant from one another. There had never been that closeness that some mums and daughters had, but she had seen me grow and become so very happy and now I had my own business that was doing well and I knew she would be devastated. I just wanted to put everything right, I didn't want her to feel any guilt about what had happened in the past.

My letter to my dad was to tell him never to walk away from the kids. I tried to explain that I did have regrets that we hadn't had more time together when we were younger, but we had what we had and I didn't want him going off the rails if anything happened to me, and him walking away from my kids now. I told him that he would always have a part of me through my kids. My memory would always live on through them.

In those last two weeks before my operation, I covered everything and everybody. The business was written down and foolproof. Tina had everything in hand, my will had been written and even the insurance companies had been made aware of what might happen. I had not stopped talking to Chris, telling him things all the time, I didn't want to leave anything out.

I hadn't been given a certain death sentence, but I was convinced that I would not be coming back and I wanted to make sure that everything and everyone was covered. I had written my letters which to me was the next best thing to writing a book that I could have done given the time I had. Chris and me must have cried buckets in those couple of weeks, but I had to say and do the things I did, I felt I needed to.

Chris was giving me all sorts of reasons to want to come back safely from the operation. He thought I was giving up, but I wasn't. I really did want to come back, believe me. He even promised me that he would take me on the honeymoon of a lifetime, because we hadn't had a honeymoon; we'd had a business to run and a family to look after.

The week before my operation I had to go to hospital for another MRI scan and MRSA swabs had to be taken, and I had a full pre-op done as well. Because it was so close to Christmas I also had all the Christmas presents bought and the tree was up. We set out all the presents under the tree and got the kids down. They thought it was great and wanted to open them there and then, but I said no. It was all done because I just wanted to see their faces and how they would have looked on Christmas morning. I even had the food ordered including the turkey.

Whatever the outcome of the operation, it was doubtful that I would be home on Christmas Day anyway. I was due to have my operation on 15th December and with Christmas only ten days later I wouldn't have been fit enough to come home, so I wanted to see my kids' reaction as they saw all their presents.

I went into hospital the night before my operation; this was to give the staff chance to complete any pre-op tests that needed doing and to get me settled. Chris took me in and when he was leaving he was very teary and so was I, but we both kept assuring each other that I would be fine.

That night I couldn't settle at all and I kept going down to the smoking shelter. It was a freezing cold night and there was snow on the ground. There were others there who had already had their operations and were recovering. They were all so jovial, but none of them had had the same procedure that I was about to have so I couldn't get any real feedback from them.

I must have gone down there a few times during the course of that night because I couldn't sleep. In the end I had to have a sleeping tablet. When I woke that morning Chris and my dad were there at the bottom of my bed. The nurse came and told me to have a shower. She said I would be going down that morning about 10 o'clock.

I went for my shower and I had only just got back when the nurse came and took my blood pressure and heart rate and stuff, then a doctor arrived and said, 'Right Jeanette, they're ready for you; you're going down now.' It was only half past eight.

My dad had just gone off down to the shelter for a smoke and Chris was with me. Normally when you're going to theatre for an operation, the person with you can come with you to the theatre, but it wasn't like that this time. I just literally walked round the corner and down a corridor and we arrived at a set of doors and Chris had to leave me there.

It is as if they do it all so quickly to save you from getting upset. One minute we are walking down the corridor together and then it's, 'Right, say goodbye, you'll see her again soon, we'll look after her.' And that's it.

We were both filling up with tears, but we hadn't time to break down before I was in there and Chris was left outside. It was to be a nine-hour operation and I knew only too well that it would be the longest nine hours of his life.

Once inside the theatre itself I couldn't believe it, there was so much equipment, it looked like life support stuff and there were so many staff. They were all over me like a rash as soon as I got in there. I wanted to ask them so many questions, but I couldn't. Nothing would come out. Before I knew it I was told I was going to be given an injection to put me out.

I'd had these things before, but this was fast. I don't think I managed to count to two and I was gone. I was having a fantastic sleep. I was in theatre for around ten hours.

The next thing I knew, I was coming round in the recovery room and I can remember screaming my head off, and I really mean screaming the place down, holding on to my head and screaming. My head was killing me, I was in agony. The nurse came to me and asked me, 'On a scale of 1 to 10 with 10 being the worst, how would you rate your pain?'

'Ten, fucking ten!' I screamed at her at the top of my voice. The doctor came and I was given some drugs to help with the pain and after a short while the same nurse asked where we were at with the pain. 'Eight.' I said.

'At least it's coming down'.

'Yes, but it's not fucking gone', I screamed back at her. I was in agony.

The doctor gave me something else for the pain. I think I heard Ketamine mentioned and I remember thinking, they give that to horses! Whatever it was they gave me must have knocked me out because the next time I woke up I was back on the ward with a nurse at my bedside taking notes. Although the pain was still there, it wasn't as bad and at least I wasn't screaming any more.

When I opened my eyes my dad was there and he was blubbing and getting hold of my hand and kissing me all over my face saying, 'Oh sweetheart, sweetheart are you all right?' and I was saying, 'Leave me alone, where's Chris?'

Dad told me Chris was on his way, but all I could say was he was supposed to be there and he wasn't. I don't know how long it was before he arrived, I don't think it was too long, but boy did I give it to him, and he was crying and I was getting more and more worked up and he was then trying to calm me down because it wasn't good for me to be that worked up after having major brain surgery.

He was trying to hug me and telling me to calm down and all I could say was, 'Where were you, you should have been here.' He tried to explain to me that someone had let him down at work and he had to do the job. He had tried to get back in time. He was devastated, but with it being our business he had no option but to do the work himself.

The next morning when I woke, they had sat me up a bit and at one point they thought I'd had a stroke because one side of my face had dropped. Chris looked at me and then at my dad and they called the doctor. I remember hearing them say 'We'd better get the doctor.'

The doctor came and I was sort of half-asleep, but I heard her saying, 'Jeanette ... Jeanette'.

I said 'Yeah.'

'Give us a smile Jeanette.' I gave them a big cheesy grin and the doctor laughed at the face I pulled, then she said, 'No she's all right; the muscles in her face moved up when she smiled, she's OK.'

That afternoon my consultant, Dr Gurusinghe was called in. He came and even though I was half-asleep and my eyes were shut, I could hear what he was saying, 'Oh yes, well she did have quite a big spinal bleed when we opened her up. If the pain continues and doesn't ease, we may need to go back in and put a shunt in.' He was describing where the shunt would go and what it would achieve. I was listening to all this with my eyes closed.

He came up to me and said, 'Jeanette, you do know that I am going away tonight, don't you? I'm going to be away for four weeks. I will be passing you over to another consultant. He is good, hopefully you won't need him; but he's there to look after you if you do need him.'

As the days went on I began to feel better and by the third day I was up and walking about. I remember thinking to myself, 'Hey! Look at me three days after brain surgery and I'm up and walking about, my head's stuck in this position and I can't move it, but hey; I'm all right ... Take me for a fag!'

Chris said 'No way, you can't have a cigarette.'

I said 'I am and I'm going for one.' But I soon realised it wasn't such a good idea; I had massive head pains again.

They had already told me that I might be able to go home after six days, which was great because it meant I would be home in time for Christmas, but on the fourth day after my surgery, during the evening I had started feeling very tired and I was having some really severe head pains.

The doctor said I had to have a lumbar puncture. As soon as they took it the doctor told me that it wasn't as it should be. He said it was very red; almost blood colour. He said he had expected to find some blood in there, but not as red as this. It was almost pure blood. He sent it off to the lab to be tested.

The microbiologist's report came back and they suspected meningitis, so they put me on a course of Meropenum which is a drug to combat meningitis. I quickly began to show some improvement, and then I was up and down for the next few days. I had built my hopes for being home for Christmas, but now I was stuck here like this.

When Christmas Eve arrived I managed to con them into letting me home just for Christmas Day. They said I would have to go back every few hours to have the Meropenum drug injected into me to help the fight against meningitis and I agreed. Chris came and picked me up that evening and I spent Christmas Eve in my own bed but on Christmas morning I knew I wasn't well enough to be there. I was sat on the settee and feeling awful. I could see the kids and everyone looking at me with their presents half-open and I realised I shouldn't be putting them through that.

I wasn't helping anyone to have a good time by being there like that and when I asked Chris to run me back to the hospital, he completely agreed with me. He could see it was the best thing for me and he took me back. I shuffled through the snow in my slippers to the car and Chris took me back to the Royal Preston Hospital.

As soon as I got back all the doctors were rushing around me; they could see I wasn't well. I had simply over-done it; I'd tried to do too much too soon – typical of me!

Chris said he would be back later and that he would bring me some Christmas pud, as I love Christmas pudding. The doctors just gave me some more of the Meropenum and ordered me to bed rest and monitored me every half hour. The rest of Christmas Day was nothing more than a blur.

The following week I grew stronger by the day and I was allowed home in time for New Year's Eve. When I got home I went straight to bed, but that only lasted about ten minutes and then my nosy head came on. As soon as I heard the door go I wanted to know who that was. I actu-ally felt fine so I got up. Later that day Chris asked what I wanted to do that night, but I don't think he had in mind what I was going to answer.

'It's New Year, I want to go out tonight to the pub.'

'Are you mad? You can't go out; you've just come home after having major brain surgery.'

I told him I was fine, it was New Year's Eve and I wanted to bring in the New Year and hope to God that it's a better one. I was adamant I was going, and we went!

I walked down to the nearest pub. I had earphones in to protect me from the noise of the traffic, because the noise set my balance off and I had a shaved head. I really didn't look the part, but I went. We sat in a corner and the music was blaring out. I lasted until about eleven and then we went home, but I had done it and I had proved a point.

19

Cleaner schools

Going back to around the time I was pregnant with the twins, I'd been thinking about what I could do to make a difference. I wanted it to be something that would give me the chance to give something back. That night I had a dream; I woke up and suddenly thought, Oh my God! I have just had an idea that could get me that OBE. It's amazing how your subconscious still works even when you're fast asleep.

I came up with something called 'Cleaner Schools'. I'd done some research into the way cleaners worked. There was a set formula for what cleaners should be capable of doing, and it was: each cleaner should be able to clean 34 square metres per hour. There were other directives for tables, shelves and glass to be cleaned.

We occasionally had to go into schools to cover work that was being done by County direct or by the schools direct, and when we had been in there and had done the clean in our own way we continually got good feedback from teachers, saying how spotless it was after we'd done the job. I quickly realised that this was what schools wanted.

I came up with the idea of offering the schools that used us a better service and a standard of cleaning that was superior. I designed a 'Cleaner Schools' logo, and planned it that all schools that took on the challenge could have the logo on the bottom of their letterheaded paper, rather like the ones that state 'Healthy Schools'. This was based on our higher level of cleaning and if anyone had this standard behind them it would have meant their school would have had a higher than average standard of cleanliness.

I knew that it was possible to clean 34 square metres per hour and still be able to clean the tables every day, the ledges every day and everything else everyday. So I spoke to a lot of people and worked with my marketing lady to design a special logo, and she also designed a website for it.

I then decided it would make sense to have all the kids involved. I went around to all the schools that used us and told them of the plan. It was for each school to come up with ideas for how they could help their school to be the cleanest. I got the kids to design posters and leaflets and had the winning posters printed and put up all over the schools.

Some of the posters said things like, 'Hang your coat up on the hooks provided' or 'Tidy all books away': simple things like that, but by getting the kids to do those small tasks, it gave my cleaners more time when they went in to concentrate on the serious stuff.

The competition was amazing. Kids are always up for any kind of a challenge. It was the site supervisor's job to go into every classroom every day and give marks for the tidiest room. Then at the end of each week the winning class got a certificate and at the end of each term, the class with the most certificates won a prize and believe me, they all wanted to win.

We would send lots of goodies to the winning school and I remember one term a school that was a special school for children with learning disabilities had won. They sent us pictures of all the kids out on the field eating chocolate cake and having a great time. They sent us a letter thanking us for their presents. It was great fun and so good to see the kids enjoying themselves.

I worked hard on this throughout 2009 and the 'Cleaner Schools' website went live, and there was an awful lot of interest from schools wanting to get involved. I thought of setting up a franchise, but at the same time I didn't want to get too big too quickly. I had taken all this on and I was still running around doing my own work as well as looking after Chris and the kids, and being pregnant. I thought to myself, 'Jeanette, you're an absolutely loopy woman, how the hell did you come up with all this?'

I wanted schools to be involved, but it was becoming too much for me to handle. I could manage running it in the schools we were already in, but for it to get any bigger, it meant I wouldn't be able to monitor it. So I did contact a number of franchise agencies, but to do this would have been very costly and very time-consuming.

Then later on, around early 2010 and because of all the interest from schools, Lancashire County Council had become interested and wanted to know how they could use it. I began to draw up a plan to work out how the County could give the award out to the schools and monitor it, with a cost for all the equipment and stationery and the rights to use it.

I had become quite excited with the idea, but things happened and the project took a sour turn. Sadly, I have decided to shelve it for the time being, but maybe it will be something I might consider for the future. I had more than enough to contend with, with being pregnant with twins and later finding out I needed brain surgery.

20

Conclusion: now and the future

Here we are at the end of 2011 and I am still not out of the woods as far as my brain surgery goes. I may still need some more work doing. I am still having head pains and the neurologist has said that I may need to have a shunt put in there. The problem seems to be an obstruction to the flow of fluid in my brain.

But I am now in a much happier place in terms of the way I look at life. I am still scared, but I suppose that is normal, considering everything. So much has happened to me in my life that I am always wondering what life is going to throw at me next. However, if life has taught me anything, it is that we shouldn't dwell too much on what has happened in the past, because there is nothing we can do to change what has gone before, but there are two things we can do. Those are: learn from it and secondly, we can (with God's help) manage our future.

I am living proof that if you have that fight within yourself you can achieve your goals. The first twenty-one years of my life were filled with bad experiences, and lots of them. The poverty that our family went through and the domestic violence would have been enough to destroy some people, but on top of all that I had bullying, drugs and sexual abuse to deal with. I felt in some ways that I didn't have the childhood other kids have.

Thanks to my neighbour, I was no longer an innocent child who didn't know about intimate things. He had made sure that I was well aware of the things adults did. He had plied me as a child with goodies and with the promise of lots of gifts and money that I knew I hadn't a hope in hell's chance of having unless I went along with his perverted games, and at that age, that was all I ever considered them to be – games!

As a child I was very small, always feeling low. I walked around with my head down everywhere I went. I was very vulnerable and an easy target for these predators that target kids. They know exactly how to read the signals. There are lots of vulnerable kids out there who will fall into the very same trap that I did, and we all need to wake up and be looking for the tell-tale signs: my mum had no idea what was going on. I was one of the lucky ones because I lived to tell the tale.

Then at the age of twelve I met my first boyfriend who went on to become my first husband. Another massive mistake! But like all teenagers you think you know best and before you know it you are in a situation whereby you are trapped. But I eventually got out of that trap by the skin of my teeth.

Then I met my Chris – what a contrast; how can life change, how can people be so vastly different? Chris is the gentlest, kindest person I have ever known and he has turned my life around. Oh, don't get me wrong, there have been many other people who have helped along the way. The last ten years have been a path of discovery and hope, for both me and for Chris. This period has truly changed the lives of us both.

All of this hasn't been easy and has come at a cost of codeine addiction for ten years of my life, but I've battled through this and may make it a subject for another book – who knows what next?

My life has indeed been a book of two halves and I

sometimes wonder if the man upstairs is setting me challenges. It is as if he is making me continually prove myself in order to keep my place, and I do keep proving my place!

My life has been one long fight. I believe that we all have the ability to fight back, but we have to want to. Once you take the first step towards finding a better life, you will find that there are lots of people out there who are willing to help you. All you have to do is ask for that help. I asked and I got.

In one way, I feel that the bad things that have happened in my life have made me stronger; they have helped to make me the woman I am today. I consider myself to be a loving, caring person. I am understanding and considerate towards others. Some people find it strange that I have turned out the way I have after all that has happened to me. I suppose I could so very easily have gone the other way.

One of the main reasons for me writing this book is that I hope it will help other women to find their way in life. Bullying and abuse are rife and for many of us who are in that situation, it becomes a part of everyday life, and we so very easily become accepting of it. Let me tell you, it doesn't need to be a part of your life; you deserve better!

Fear is the biggest thing. Having to fight to be strong and to find a way forward or a way out of a bad situation is the thing. Once you make that first move, you can begin to focus and look forward. What you must do from then on is train your brain to continue to focus and look forward. As soon as you feel the benefits, you will grow stronger. If you allow your negative thoughts to win, you are allowing the bullies to win.

The realisation of knowing who and what your problems are, is the first step, and secondly you need to find a purpose in life that will help you to keep that focus. For me it was keeping me occupied, i.e. my work as a cleaner, a partner and a mother. You may already have the reason for that focus – you may have children. Do you want a better life for them?

I didn't get through this on my own though, my problems involved a lot of mental health issues such as my PTSD and for that I needed qualified help, but I took those steps and got that help. It wasn't easy and at times I very nearly gave up. My health reached its lowest point and it took some straight talking from my doctor before I began to question myself.

I hadn't believed him at first, but the more I considered his words the more it began to make sense. It is when you start to look at yourself and question yourself, your actions and the way your brain works that you truly begin to find the answers. But you must have the courage to do that. When I go to my doctor now if I am feeling down, he simply says to me, 'Jeanette, c'mon, you know what you have to do.' And he's right!

My life changed and I changed too. The more focused I became the stronger I became as a person. I began to look at life so differently. I questioned every thought that came into my head and I knew I had to keep negative thoughts well away. I had come so far and there is no way I was going to allow myself to slip back to those dark days again.

There are days when I feel down and there always will be, but I have to remind myself that life is so much better here and now, and I am not going to let the grey mist come down over me. I want these good feelings every day, not just for me, but for my Chris and for our five beautiful children. I now have a lovely home, five wonderful children and a successful business. A few years ago I had nothing.

By looking at the way my brain works and knowing all the telltale signs of depression, I can lift myself and Chris and the kids from the gloom. I can tell if my darling Emma is low and needs a boost that day, and I know how to lift her. Chris too knows when he is feeling low and he now knows how to handle his problems.

It is all about finding your own niche, and discovering what works best for you as an individual. Fear of making that first move is what scares us all, but there are people out there to help you. You will not be alone, and often the thing we fear most is ourselves – the fear of failing!

Doing my college course on criminology taught me so much. I learned how to understand how others think. I began to analyse everyone and every situation, and that made me realise that I couldn't allow them to win. We can spend years picking up the pieces, but if we can find our way out of bad situations we can overcome anything. Let's show these people that they're not going to win, let us show them what we've become from them.

I hope this book will help those of you who have been, or are, in a brutish relationship or have experienced poverty and abuse. If I can help just one person to find a better life for themselves, then all this will have been worthwhile.

My life has been hell, but I honestly believe that all the bad things in my life have contributed to my being the strong person I am today: everything that has happened to me, including my childhood, my violent marriage to Blake and more recently my brain surgery. If I can turn my life around, so can you.

Believe in yourself! Get help and kickstart your new life today.